SAY PLEASE AND THANK YOU
& STAND IN LINE

SAY PLEASE
AND THANK YOU
& STAND IN LINE

One Man's Story of
What Makes Canada Special,
And How to Keep It That Way

DANY ASSAF

sh.
SUTHERLAND
HOUSE

Sutherland House
416 Moore Ave., Suite 205
Toronto, ON M4G 1C9

First edition, May 2021

If you are interested in inviting one of our authors to a live event or
media appearance, please contact matt@sutherlandhousebooks.com and
visit our website at sutherlandhousebooks.com for more information
about our authors and their schedules.

Manufactured in Canada
Cover designed by Lena Yang
Book composed by Carmen Siu

Library and Archives Canada Cataloguing in Publication

Title: Say please and thank you & stand in line : one man's story of what
makes Canada special, and how to keep it that way / Dany Assaf.
Other titles: Say please and thank you and stand in line
Names: Assaf, Dany H., author.
Identifiers: Canadiana 20200380974 | ISBN 9781989555378 (softcover)
Subjects: LCSH: Assaf, Dany H. | LCSH: Muslims—Canada—Biography.
| LCSH: Muslims—Canada—Social conditions. | LCSH: Religious
discrimination—Canada. | LCSH: Racism—Canada. | LCSH: Lawyers—
Canada—Biography. | LCSH: Canada—Race relations. | LCSH:
Canada—Ethnic relations. | LCGFT: Autobiographies.
Classification: LCC FC106.M9 A87 2021 | DDC 305.6/970971—dc23

ISBN 978-1-989555-37-8

*To my wife Lisa, my other half, and my children Mohamad,
Danya, Zain, and Hannah, and my parents and siblings
for all your love and loyalty.*

*To the memory of my great-grandfather
and the path he and many like him forged.*

To all my friends who blessed my life.

To everyone who has made Canada so special.

Contents

Prologue

I'S OFTEN SAID THAT HOCKEY IS A RELIGION in Canada, but on Monday, June 17 in 2019, it was a basketball team that called the city to worship. I rushed from my office through the pedestrian walkways beneath Toronto's business district, making my way towards city hall and Nathan Phillips Square. I was meeting with my family: none of us wanted to miss out on history. The usually bustling underground walkways were eerily empty; everyone else was already out in the street, two million people lined up to celebrate the Toronto Raptors and their NBA championship. I finally emerged from the subterranean maze into the sunshine of the square and found myself amid a sea of ecstatic people, a crowd as diverse as it was deep.

It was a once-in-a-lifetime event. Perhaps there were echoes of the celebrations that followed the 1972 Canada/Russia hockey summit, but those scenes, which took place almost fifty years ago, would have looked very different. The complexion of contemporary Toronto is unique. It is now the most multicultural city in the world, with 230 nationalities and 140 languages, and I'm sure every single one of them was in Nathan Phillips Square as the Raptors arrived on the team bus.

It is one thing to read statistics about Toronto's remarkable diversity in race, religion, and nationality, and quite another to find yourself in a moment where you are completely immersed in it. The *New York Times* ran an article under the headline "The Raptors Win, and Canada Learns to Swagger" and captured the moment with these words: in addition to all those ball caps, "there were turbans and hijabs... Everyone was represented, and everyone was representing... Never before had I felt more connected to our flag."

It occurred to me that one reason this hockey town had so wholeheartedly embraced a basketball team was that the Raptors themselves had one of the most diverse lineups in professional sport. No matter who you were, you could see a piece of yourself to cheer for. The roster included a Cameroonian, a Congolese, a Spaniard, an American of Taiwanese descent, a Brit born of Nigerian parents, a Montrealer, and several Americans. The Raptors' American coach, Nick Nurse, summed it up this way: "I tell everybody this all the time. This place is unique. I'm kind of an international guy, I've lived in a few countries and I kind of like the spirit of the cultural diversity here in Toronto, in our organization and our staff, the team."

The Toronto Maple Leafs might have deeper roots in local history, but the Raptors represented the new Toronto, indeed, the new Canada, and what can be accomplished when many come together as one. While we were out there celebrating our team's victory on June 17, we were also celebrating ourselves.

The day was not perfect. Four people were shot near Nathan Phillips Square (all fortunately survived) and we had also just come out of a contentious provincial election which was surrounded by what has now become the usual election circus atmosphere, including some divisive arguments over immigrants. These tensions were reminders that we are always vulnerable to succumbing to our fears and letting our worst instincts dictate how the world works.

Now, with the world as it is, it feels like history is calling us to either harness the power of our multicultural assets, socially and economically, at home and on the world stage, or be torn apart by our differences. One need not look far to see what happens when one faction or sect portrays another as the enemy. Sometimes it feels we are in a time when our narcissism is in combat with our willingness to listen to others, leaving little space for us to grow and learn from one another. The consequences are not only the lost opportunities to genuinely fix what's fallen apart but also the mistrust, injustice, and oppression, and sometimes violence and death, that this division can bring.

My family's story encompasses moments of otherness, but it mostly speaks to the incredible inclusivity of Canada. That June morning, spent celebrating the Raptors and their victory, reaffirmed for me why Canada remains a special place in a messy world. However, my path through life has shown me enough to never take that special quality for granted. I would never have believed, for instance, that our neighbour to the south could degenerate so quickly into incivility, sanctioned by the highest office in the land. I worry what would await future generations of Canadians if we spend our days trying to find meaning in ourselves through anger at the "other."

We must resist. Genuine progress needs to be anchored by trust, mutual respect, and consensus. That is the path to prosperity; the other leads to ruin. Canada, however imperfect, has been as welcoming to diverse peoples as any country on the face of the earth, with so many wonderful results. I've written this book in the hopes that we continue to build on the finest of our heritage—what I like to call the Canadian way—and never lose sight of what is best in us.

PART I
FAMILY MATTERS

Chapter One

The Enemy Within

"OSAMA BIN LADEN LIVES CLOSER THAN YOU THINK." After the tragedy of 9/11, this sign appeared on an Edmonton lawn with an arrow pointing to my parents' house. They lived at the end of a quiet cul-de-sac; no one would see the sign except the few families who lived there. It was another neighbour, Bill, who first saw it. A middle-aged father and a religious man, Bill was so concerned he drove to the police station rather than just call. Bill told my parents to stay in the house and to make sure my brothers didn't go out until the police arrived. He wanted to shield my parents from seeing the sign, and he was worried something violent might happen.

The neighbour who put up the sign was a middle-aged single mother with a teenaged son. As a boy, the son would come home from school and let himself in; his mother was still at work. On one cold Edmonton winter day, my brother Sid noticed the boy, who was nine or ten years old at the time, standing outside his house. It was freezing. Sid asked him what was wrong. His key didn't work. He was standing out there, shivering. Sid invited him to come into our house and wait.

Our house was like a hotel. We were six kids: my four brothers, Aumer, Sid, Sammir and Belal, and my sister Summer. We always had friends over. My mother, Gada, loved having everyone there.

As I got older, I began to appreciate how much work it was for my mother to look after all of us and our countless friends. I remember once asking her how she always had the energy to do that for us. Simply because she loved us, she answered, and hoped that with six kids in a big world, wherever her children went, they would also find someone to welcome them. She believed in paying it forward. In fact, wherever I have gone in this big world, I have always found warm people to welcome me. I also remember a great line she would use on us when we couldn't get her permission to do something that she thought was dangerous or risky, and she wanted to protect us. She would say, "Better you cry a day than I cry a lifetime." I use that on my kids to this day. This is the person who welcomed that boy on that cold winter day.

When his mother got back from work, she came over, grateful we'd taken her son in. She stayed for dinner. My mother said, "Listen, from now on, every day he comes here until you get home." So he came over all the time. He'd sit and watch TV, have a Coke or a chocolate bar. Like a member of the family.

Those years of being a good neighbour vanished instantly in the wake of 9/11. The sign on her lawn went up within weeks. When the police arrived, one officer went to my parents' door and the other went to the neighbour's. By then, she had taken the sign down. My mother was crying, and the officer asked, "Did your neighbour bring on these tears?" He immediately left to join his partner. The officers found the sign in the garage. There wasn't enough to charge her with a hate crime, but the police warned her that they would hand out potential charges if she put the sign back up.

The sign never went back up, but the heat never came down. It wouldn't be the last time the police were called. After 9/11, things were never the same. My parents and brothers, born and bred Albertans, had been labelled terrorists.

This neighbour had a brother who was often at her house. He was big, loud, aggressive, a natural bully. He would get in his car, pull up in front of our house and shine his high beams into our living room and honk his horn. It felt like a home invasion. My brothers, who, like me, had grown up playing a lot of hockey, wanted to go out and confront him. I worried it could escalate into violence. The neighbour's brother brought thuggish friends over and they taunted my father, trying to get him to fight. They threatened my mother. My brothers, in their twenties at the time and living downtown, would have to race home to deal with this. The neighbour, the same person whose son we had taken in and helped nurture, stood behind her brother, egging him on like a cheerleader. For months my family lived in this charged atmosphere of inexplicable hatred and the threat of violence. The police would come on occasion, but their hands were tied, they said. The brother hadn't done anything expressly illegal. My mother was terrified.

It's extraordinary that three thousand kilometres from Ground Zero, a terrorist attack could pit neighbour against neighbour in the otherwise placid suburb of a foreign country. Some neighbours, like Bill and his wife Susan, rallied to support my parents. Others didn't, and some didn't get involved. The incident turned the street into a psychological warzone for months as tensions escalated. The neighbour or her brother cut down Bill and Susan's shrubs, which bordered their own yard. Whenever my parents left their house, there was the possibility of an unpleasant encounter with her or the brother. Visitors who parked too close to them were ambushed.

They were all unpleasant, but the brother was potentially violent. One evening when I was visiting my parents, the brother once more drove up to their house and shone his high beams into the living room while revving his engine. It was a disturbing gesture. He finally stopped, and I watched him park and sit in his car for a few minutes then walk into his sister's house. The next morning, I told him and his sister to knock it off. My brothers knew that he was trying to goad them into doing something so he could retaliate against them. They didn't rise to the bait.

My parents were married in 1968 and have only lived in three different homes in Edmonton. They always thought it was critical to provide us with stability, keep us in the same schools, and provide a loving, supportive home life. My father described his children like beautiful flowers in the garden; it may be possible to transplant them from one garden to another but there was always a risk that their roots wouldn't take hold as strongly in a new place. But this awful experience made him think about moving. The terror lasted for months. The woman tried to recruit the neighbours to her side, tried to demonize my parents. She demanded to know whether they were all blind to the terrorist threat next door. My parents had been on the street longer than anyone, had forged relationships with many of the neighbours. My brothers and I had grown up playing ball hockey with kids on the street. We all felt we were a version of Wayne Gretzky. I had never imagined that we could ever be viewed as a version of Osama bin Laden.

This episode reminded me of a story I had read about the collapse of Yugoslavia, when Sarajevo turned into a war zone; in a short time, Sarajevo went from hosting the 1984 Winter Olympics to hosting one of the bloodiest civil wars in recent history. During these war years, there was a mailman who killed an entire Muslim family. The family had owned a restaurant, and the mailman regularly ate there and delivered mail to them. The point of the story was that nothing unimaginable had happened that drove him to kill this family. In certain extreme cases, regular people can do horrible things when reckless and shameless leaders force them to choose sides. Instead, here was the banality of evil. He didn't have any tangible reason to do what he did. There was just something in the cultural air that compelled him. It was a tragedy that victimized all its citizens.

Fortunately, Canadian society is more resilient and enlightened. My aggressive neighbour was increasingly ostracized by everyone else on the street, and one day she mercifully moved away. We never saw her or her brother again. But the damage was done; we suddenly felt vulnerable. And it raised a disturbing question that hadn't been asked before in our family: did this represent something that had always been beneath the surface?

In the wake of 9/11, there was rhetoric that made some people feel they had to pick sides, and that they had social license to express hate against an entire religion, to "fight back" in a misguided battle against almost two billion fellow humans on this shrinking planet. The reality of 9/11 is that this event took innocent lives from every religion and background. Those planes did not ask anyone's faith before they crashed into the Twin Towers. Muslim Canadians mourned victims of the attack and were mortified and angry that this gang of criminals would try to hijack an entire faith. The pain of watching this double nightmare unfold was maddening and infused with helplessness. When I look back on that episode, it looks like a leading indicator of the discord and hate that now seems to be spreading.

*

Two years after 9/11, I found myself at the end of a long boardroom table in Toronto asking a surreal question to the editorial board of the *Globe and Mail*: "Which of my children do you imagine giving me a suicide belt for Father's Day?"

I was there because the *Globe* had published a cartoon showing a generic Arab boy joyously giving his father a suicide belt as a Father's Day gift. No commentary, just a straight-up stereotype vilifying an entire race in our national newspaper, a Canadian institution. It was a surprise, and it felt like a betrayal. It challenged my notion of citizenship.

My Muslim great-grandfather came to Edmonton from Lebanon in 1927 to join other Muslims who had made the prairies their home since the 1890s. The Muslim community wasn't large, but it was significant and well-integrated. We were Albertan and Canadian and felt a deep sense of belonging in every way. We never imagined we could be vilified as the "other." But seventy-six years later, someone was questioning whether I belonged. Canada, filled with people whose roots literally cover the globe, is a collection of similar stories. If one story can be thrown aside in a moment, could others?

After seeing the cartoon, I called the newspaper and demanded a meeting with the editor. Before the meeting, I thought about how I could convey the illogical and deeply personal impact this had on our fellow Canadians of Arab descent. On my credenza there was a picture of my son Mohamad and my daughter Danya. They were maybe three and two at the time, wearing little sunglasses on a sunny Toronto day. I grabbed the photo on my way out of my office. When I got to the *Globe*, I started the meeting by sliding the photograph across the length of the boardroom table and asking that absurd question.

The point was made, an apology of sorts offered. But it was an unsettling experience to see a racist stereotype endorsed in a national newspaper. I wondered how we had gotten to this moment, and where we were headed at the dawn of the twenty-first century. It was light years away from my childhood, growing up as a Muslim on the Canadian prairies.

Growing up in Edmonton in the 1970s, I lived for hockey. One of my most vivid childhood memories is my father taking me to Sport Chek when I was four to buy my first jersey and set of hockey gear.

The dream of playing in the NHL lived in me. In some delusional way, it still lives in me. Hockey provided my first sense of belonging to a team, my community, my country. The fathers in the community took turns looking after the neighbourhood outdoor rink, and my father was one of them. I would watch him do the final evening flood to ensure there was a nice sheet of ice to play on the next morning. To this day, the sight or memory of a clean sheet of ice under a big blue prairie sky stirs up an almost spiritual feeling deep inside.

There is a beauty to the game, though it isn't always played that way. But it provided me with valuable lessons. The first is that we are all vulnerable. We are moving fast on thin, sharp metal blades, carrying sticks. At some point, everyone's back is to the play. You can be blindsided, hammered into the boards. Even the biggest and toughest aren't safe. So there are rules. For me this captures an aspect of Canadian culture—chaos may prevail briefly in volatile circumstances, but ultimately peace, order, and good government endures. That is the fabric that holds the country together.

When asked what I do, I sometimes respond that I'm a failed hockey player who became a lawyer. I moved to Toronto for law school and grew to be part of its vaunted diverse landscape. I became a lawyer in a Bay Street firm, with a wife, four children, a member of clubs, still playing hockey (perhaps unwisely), part of the establishment.

But in the wake of 9/11, after the towers fell, I was potentially The Other, and that Father's Day *Globe* cartoon in 2003 brought this home to me in a very stark way. The narrative had changed. Narrative is a powerful force, and it can overtake history, facts, logic, and individual lives. When the story changed, it took me a while before I realized they could be talking about me.

*

That narrative gained momentum in 2006, when an alleged Muslim terrorist plot was uncovered in Toronto. The Toronto 18, as they came to be called, planned to storm both the Canadian Broadcasting Centre in Toronto and the Parliament buildings in Ottawa, in order to take hostages and ultimately behead the Prime Minister and others. The scale and horror of the planned violence captured the imagination of the public. The night after the arrests, two Toronto mosques were attacked. Newspapers described the accused as "brown-skinned young men." John Hostettler, Chairman of the House Subcommittee on Border Security in the United States, announced, "South Toronto was an enclave for radical discussion" and had "a militant understanding of Islam." Put aside the fact that "South Toronto" doesn't exist as a district, the comments were alarmist and without any evidence whatsoever. But they were powerful enough to eclipse a century of Muslim contributions in almost every corner of the country.

The "Toronto 18" turned out to be a misnomer: six had their charges stayed and one had his charges dismissed. They turned out to be incompetent and disorganized (described by a defense lawyer as a "hapless F-troop"), but the spectre of organized terrorism didn't disappear. Their goals were murky ("Rome has to be defeated") and their ties to existing terror groups non-existent. Their court appearances had police snipers on rooftops, and the police had a nickname for the teenagers involved: "the jihad generation." I don't want to downplay the seriousness of what could have happened and what these criminals intended, but this group constituted 11 men in a Muslim population of more than a million in Canada, with a century of contribution to the country. Nevertheless, the narrative swept up an entire religion into the story it wanted to tell. The effects of that narrative still linger today.

*

A decade later, the narrative got darker still. In January 2017, a man approached the Islamic Cultural Centre in Quebec City just as evening prayers had ended. He pointed a semi-automatic rifle toward two men who were leaving and pulled the trigger. The rifle jammed, and he pulled out a 9 mm Glock pistol and shot the two men. He entered the mosque and continued shooting. In less than two minutes he killed six men and critically injured five others. One of the men he killed, Azzeddine Soufiane, a 57-year-old grocery store owner, rushed the gunman in an attempt to disarm him. He was posthumously awarded a medal for bravery by the Quebec government. The shooter fled the mosque, then turned himself over to police twenty minutes later.

He was charged with six counts of first-degree murder and six counts of attempted murder (the sixth referring to the 35 other people in the mosque). At the trial it was revealed that he'd been a follower of right-wing U.S. figures such as former Klan leader David Duke, and neo-Nazi and white supremacist Richard Spencer. In the days before the shooting, he had repeatedly visited U.S. President Donald Trump's Twitter feed. Trump had just imposed a ban on visitors from Muslim countries. The shooter told the police he was afraid his family would be attacked by Islamic terrorists. Francois Huot, judge for the Quebec Superior Court, said that "His crimes were truly motivated by race, and a visceral hatred toward Muslim immigrants." The shooter was sentenced to forty years in prison. Both the crown and defense appealed the sentence: one felt it was too lenient, the other too harsh.

Several thousand people attended a vigil for those who died in the attack. This outpouring of support was gratifying, but it didn't change the underlying tensions that existed in the province. For more than a decade, successive Quebec governments have tried to regulate religious dress, the hijab and niqab in particular.

While the shooting was a truly horrifying attack on this mosque, it wasn't the only incident. In 2016, a pig's head was left outside the building during Ramadan. In the year of the shooting, hate crimes tripled against Quebec City's 10,000 Muslims. The mosque shooter confessed to a social worker that he regretted he hadn't killed more Muslims. It was an unprecedented horror in a Canadian house of worship, but the larger fear was that now a precedent had been set.

On March 15, 2019, a man killed fifty-one people and injured forty-nine others in two mosques in Christchurch, New Zealand. At the first, the Al Noor Mosque, he was greeted with the words, "Hello, brother." Like the shooter at the Charleston, South Carolina church in 2015, whose victims welcomed him to pray with them before he shot them dead, this killer shot that man and dozens more during the course of Friday prayer. He cited Norwegian terrorist Anders Behring Breivik as inspiration, and said he supported President Trump as "a symbol of renewed white identity and common purpose."

The fears after this horror were manifold. There was the scale and hatred of the attack, which left the country shaken. It was noted that hate crimes against Muslims had already been on the rise. The invocation of Trump was unsettling as well, since it appeared that the idea of a brand of identity politics based on exclusion or the oppression of a minority was now gaining mainstream legitimacy.

Three months after the Christchurch massacre, the issue of Muslim terrorism came up in a Canadian parliamentary justice committee. Michael Cooper, the Conservative MP for St. Albert-Edmonton and the Deputy Shadow Minister for Justice, was removed from the committee for berating a Muslim anti-racist witness who was testifying before the committee. Faisal Khan Suri of Edmonton noted that the killers in the Quebec shooting, the Pittsburgh synagogue shooting that killed eleven people, and the Christchurch murders were all influenced by hate promoted by "alt-right online networks." Cooper told Suri that he "should be ashamed of himself" for linking the murders to conservatism, then read part of the Christchurch killer's manifesto (banned in New Zealand, although Cooper had a copy with him) into the official record to make his point.

In the wake of Cooper's performance, two of his former law school colleagues came forward and said that as a student, Cooper had argued that Islam had no place in Canada. Cooper denied the charge, but Balqees Mihirig, a lawyer practising in New York, wrote that Cooper had said Canada's "Judeo-Christian civilization" was incompatible with "goat-herder cultures."

The bigger question for me was how one of our national representatives could be so ignorant about the history of the land under his feet. Cooper was the MP for St. Albert, a northern suburb of Edmonton that sits on the highway headed north. A century earlier, the first Muslim immigrants to Canada, including my great-grandfather, practically wore out that road as they traded fur and goods in Northern Alberta and put down roots in places like Lac La Biche, Fort Chipewyan, and Frog Lake.

The cost of this new, frightening narrative was impossible to measure. What is the effect on a generation of Muslim children who feel like "the other?" When a culture of fear takes root, it is difficult to turn it around. How did Canada get here and who is next?

On September 12, 2020, Mohamed-Aslim Zafis, a 58-year-old volunteer at the International Muslim Organization mosque in Toronto, was murdered by a man wearing a hoodie. Zafis was standing outside the mosque for evening prayer, making sure everyone obeyed the COVID-19 protective protocols, when a man walked up to him and slit his throat. Police investigated it as a potential hate crime. They also wondered if it was linked to another murder, a man in his thirties named Rampreet Singh, who had been living under a bridge. That murder had happened only days earlier, about four kilometres away in north Toronto. Bernie Farber, Chair of the Canadian Anti-Hate Network, said that "We're seeing an increase in hate that is relatively unprecedented. The three groups that are most targeted are Jews, Muslims and people of colour."

As Farber noted, people came to the mosque seeking peace. It was a turbulent, stressful time. Businesses were failing, people losing jobs, children that would normally be in school or daycare were at home. In turbulent, stressful times, some people seek peace, and others look for someone to blame.

On October 12, an ominous message was received at a downtown Toronto mosque. It threatened to "do a Christ church" and predicted that "The police will take our side. Islam will not defeat us. We have the guns to do a Christchurch all over again..." The Toronto Police Service was called to investigate and the mosque was closed to worshippers. The National Council of Canadian Muslims, the Centre for Israel and Jewish Affairs, and two-dozen other faith groups came together to demand the government take stronger measures to combat domestic hate groups.

Some of the seeds of this interfaith cooperation were sown at a unique dinner that my wife Lisa and I hosted for leaders of the Canadian Muslim and Jewish communities to get to know one another. It was an incredible evening that allowed everyone to meet and have an honest discussion around our dinner table. We learned a lot about one another's communities. I referred to it as a "family dinner," because family dinners are the time when everyone feels safe to share their fears and hopes. While we may not have agreed on Middle-East politics, we shared a common cause in protecting our Canadian way of life in the face of new threats. A Canada that does not protect its Muslim and Jewish citizens is not only bad for Muslims and Jews, but would also cease to represent the Canada so many others have fought and sacrificed for in our history.

In my work as a competition lawyer, I travel extensively, and I see firsthand the creeping nationalism, populism, and isolationism in the world, all the isms that are damaging to the economy and trade. This has created even more anxiety among vulnerable populations, with some political leaders capitalizing on that anxiety and stoking fears that "the other" has taken their job, their prosperity, their future, thereby changing their way of life. Everyone is somehow being taken advantage of. Diversity is now an enemy.

It is both sad and ironic that our most compelling response to complex technological disruption and innovation is to revert to base tribal instincts and attack one another. Barriers to trade are going up, and borders are hardening to keep "the other" out. The order that we created in a post-World War II global community is in jeopardy. Our caveman ancestors would be proud.

Not only are these pressures fraying our social fabric, they are also weakening our economic potential. Social cohesion promotes an inclusive economy, and an inclusive economy provides opportunity and prosperity for all. It's easier to stay happier and healthier when we are all wealthier.

Sadly, we are losing our way at the exact moment in history when global markets and current technology are primed to reward the economic power and potential of our diversity. Ironically, even as democracy is now under threat, economic forces and the tools of productivity are increasingly being democratized. Due to the way current technology, data, and markets are interconnected, the barriers to market entry have never been lower and an individual's ability to directly participate in the economy has never been higher. Business relationships are becoming disintermediated. Supply chains are now complex and multinational and entrenched. It is no longer possible or wise to completely shut the economic door to outsiders, whether at home or abroad. The modern economy is like a rushing river—even if you put a boulder in the middle, the water will find a way around it.

The economy is where I see hope because our social cohesion and individual economic interests have never been so directly intertwined. My ancestors came from Lebanon, and before Beirut became a symbol for devastation, it was a global trading hub. Three thousand years ago, the Phoenicians created the first global economy. They sailed around the world to trade, and other cultures came to them. As a result, merchants learned other languages, new customs. They accommodated, communicated, and prospered.

We are at the cusp of a historical moment. We can entrench ourselves in our respective ideologies and nationalisms, minimizing economic prosperity and maximizing the chances of war, or we can embrace "the other" as economic allies rather than enemies, which will lead to prosperity and peace.

Canada is one of the most diverse countries on Earth, and we are poised to profit from this global economy. It would be both tragic and ironic if, after having come all this way in our history with all the work and sacrifice of those before us, we choose this moment, an age offering the most concrete economic benefits to our diverse and inclusive mosaic, to turn our back on its greatest potential payoff for us and for future generations.

Chapter Two

Home is People

AFAVOURED TAUNT OF RACISTS, one my family has heard, is, "Go back to where you came from!" In the case of me and my brothers, that is Edmonton. Our family originally came from the Bekaa Valley in Lebanon. My great-grandfather Said (Sid) Tarrabain arrived in Edmonton in 1927. He was following in the footsteps of other Muslim Lebanese immigrants.

It is believed that the Rahal family was one of the first, arriving in 1885, the same year that the ceremonial Last Spike was driven by Donald Smith. News of the 1896 Yukon gold rush brought others from Lebanon. But news travelled slowly back then, and by the time it got to two other Lebanese adventurers in the Bekaa Valley, Sine Abouchadi and his nephew Ali Abouchadi, the gold rush was over. They arrived in northern Alberta in 1905, the year Alberta officially became part of Confederation, and five years after the gold rush had played out.

The landscape the Abouchadis found themselves in was cold and hostile, the opposite of the lush Mediterranean Bekaa Valley. Northern Alberta was sparsely treed, sparsely populated, and covered in snow half the year. There was no gold and few would immediately see it as the land of opportunity. But the Abouchadis saw opportunity there. At the time, other immigrants were starting to arrive to the West, many of them taking advantage of the government's offer of free land. There were more than a million immigrants in the course of twenty years, and those people needed supplies. The Abouchadis opened a store in Lac La Biche, 160 kilometres north of Edmonton. It was a great success, and in 1911, Mohamed Abuali Gotmi (re-named Frank Coutney) came from Lebanon to help out in the store.

Frank was an enterprising man and soon set up his own fur trading business. He learned to speak not just English and French, but also Ukrainian and Swedish, so he could speak to the newly arrived immigrants. More importantly, he learned to speak Cree and Dene, so he could trade with the Indigenous neighbours who were still heavily involved in the fur trade. Lebanon has always been a crossroads, and deeply ingrained in its culture is a respect for the power of language and commerce to forge connections. That lesson wouldn't have been lost on a farmer from Bekaa Valley, and the Abouchadis applied it in northern Alberta. Four years later, Mohamed Assaf, a cousin of my great-grandfather, came to Lac La Biche to work in the fur trade as well.

The business that had brought the French and English to Canada four centuries earlier was now attracting Lebanese immigrants. The original fur trade had languished in the mid-nineteenth century when the fad for beaver hats died in Europe, but at the beginning of the twentieth century it was revived by the demand for fur coats. The Abouchadis tapped into that demand and became very successful. Others came to join them. By 1969, the Lebanese Muslim community in Lac La Biche made up 10 percent of the town's population, the highest proportion of any town or city in North America (it's now 14 percent and, farther north, in Fort McMurray, it's 15 percent).

The Abouchadis sent back word of this new world of opportunities to their hometown of Lala in the Bekaa Valley. This was what brought Lala resident Sid Tarrabain, my great-grandfather, to Alberta. He had first tried to come after the First World War, but his ship only got as far as Genoa, Italy before turning back. After the failed Genoa voyage, his next opportunity didn't arrive until 1927. Unfortunately, his wife was six months pregnant with their son Mohammed Said. They already had a daughter, Fatima (my grandmother). It was a difficult choice to leave his family behind, but the plan, as it was for so many immigrants, was that he would go and establish himself in Canada and then send for the family. So in 1927, Sid arrived in Edmonton alone.

It was a city of 68,000 then, the former staging point for the Klondike gold rush, now settling into its role as the provincial capital. While the climate, vegetation, and history of Lala couldn't have been more different from Alberta's, they had one thing in common: they were both farming communities. There is family lore of Assaf dynasties of centuries past, but by my great-grandfather's time our family were simple farmers. And perhaps this underlying familiarity with farming life made him feel comfortable on the Prairies.

There was also the fact that farmers in my great-grandfather's village tended to be merchants as well as farmers. They had to go to Beirut to sell their produce. It was in Beirut that they got news from the outside world, and that news trickled through the population in varying degrees of reliability. For centuries, Lebanon has hosted dozens of cultures and traders. It has been ruled by Greeks, Romans, Arabs, Ottomans, and after the First World War, was under the French mandate until it achieved its independence in 1943. If nothing else, this taught the Lebanese to adapt and even thrive under any circumstances. In some ways, that ancient land was an early version of Canada, where people from different places and identities have always intersected and ultimately co-existed.

Sid opened a general store in the centre of the city, on Jasper Avenue. His cousin, Ali Tarrabain, who came to Canada around the same time, opened a store on Whyte Avenue, the other major street in Edmonton. Sid quickly built relationships across the community, as many of those early Lebanese immigrants did.

By the 1930s, there were dozens of Lebanese fur traders throughout northern Alberta and into the Northwest Territories. I had another set of relatives among this group, including my uncle, Munir Hamdon, who is still vibrant at now more than 90-years-old; he was the son of Hilwi Hamdon, who was so instrumental in building Edmonton's historic Al Rashid Mosque, the first mosque in Canada. His parents operated the general store in Fort Chipewyan and were also in the fur trading business. "There were Lebanese fur traders in every little town from Edmonton to the Arctic," Mo told me. "Fort Chipewyan, Fort McMurray, Grande Prairie, Frog Lake, Lac La Biche. Almost all of them from the Bekaa Valley, most of them somehow related."

Munir's father would supply local Indigenous neighbours with food, traps, and whatever else they needed to operate. The trappers would return with pelts, pay off their bill, and be paid for the rest. Munir's father would then sell the pelts, thousands in a single season, at the fur auction in Edmonton. If he felt the prices there were too low, he would go to Winnipeg or Montreal, or, for the best price, New York. He had contacts across the continent, an extraordinary thing for a man in such an isolated area. Fort Chipewyan had 800 people, including the RCMP officers stationed there, a radioman from the army corps, a few hundred Indigenous people, and the Hudson's Bay Company.

But while many people flourished, there could be a personal cost. Three years after arriving, my great-grandfather Sid still didn't feel he was established enough to send for his family. By the time he was ready, he received the terrible news that his wife had died. His children were too young to come over, and they stayed in Lebanon to be raised by an uncle and aunt.

*

By 1950, it was finally time for Sid to send for his son, my uncle Mohammed Said Tarrabain (later re-named Jimmy), to join him in Alberta. Jimmy was in his early twenties, and may have been the first person to come from Lala by plane. Fatima, his sister and my grandmother, stayed in Lala, got married and started her own family. It hadn't been an easy childhood for Jimmy and Fatima, and it created a very special bond between them. In many ways, she loved him as much as her own children. She was also immensely proud of the success that their father had achieved in Canada, but these feelings were mixed with sadness. Canada was also the reason that they didn't get to see their father. Because of the vast distance and the responsibilities of running his business, Sid had never been back, hadn't seen his children grow up, hadn't been able to attend his wife's funeral. But he would finally see his son, who was now a young man.

Jimmy came to Canada in August 1950 to work in the store on Jasper Avenue. He only stayed there a few months before joining his relatives in the fur trade. Sid was connected to Lac La Biche and the fur trade through his cousin, Mohamed Assaf (who would also become the first Secretary of the Arabian-Canadian Muslim Association). By the end of his first year in Canada, with the support of his father, Jimmy was in the mink ranching business in Lac La Biche.

Mink ranching had become a big business. When Frank Coutney had originally gotten into it a few decades earlier, the Dominion Bureau of Statistics reported only three mink ranches in all of Canada. But demand for fur coats grew and hundreds of fur ranching operations started in the 1920s. By 1930, there were 1,600 mink on Alberta farms. As the industry grew, standards fell. The mink were often kept in poor conditions, which yielded poor results; the coats were inferior to mink trapped in the wild. In 1936, the Alberta government built a model fur farm and experimental station for mink at the Oliver Mental Hospital outside of Edmonton, an attempt to improve the quality of mink farming.

Uncle Jimmy didn't need the government's help. His furs were winning awards across North America, receiving accolades from The Hudson Bay Company, at the Seattle Fur Exchange, the Western Canadian Raw Fur Auction, and in New York. His furs were sought after by ranches as far away as Russia. He had initially bought breeding pairs from local Indigenous neighbours, and also bought fish from them, which he fed to the mink. I can remember going up to the ranch as a child and feeding the mink. There were rows of cages in a big barn. They were vicious and Uncle Jimmy warned me to be careful feeding them or I'd lose a finger. He had learned the hard way, losing one of his own fingers when he first got into the business.

While Uncle Jimmy was setting up his new life in Lac La Biche (with a large family of 9 children including his only son Sid, who I greatly looked up to as a kid and who became a prominent lawyer in Alberta), my father, Mohamed Assaf, was still a young boy in Lala, going to school and helping with farming duties. My father was the second oldest of Fatima's eleven kids and the oldest boy, which came with many responsibilities. Lala was known for its wheat, barley, and lentil crops so he helped in the fields as well as in the family orchards of olives, grapes, figs, cherries, walnuts, almonds, and apricots. He also had to tend and milk the cows and help my grandmother around the house.

In 1959, when my father was sixteen, he left the village to go to Beirut so that he could finish high school on his own and continue his post-secondary education in accounting. At the time, Beirut was still truly the "Paris of the Middle East." It is now hard to imagine how beautiful and cosmopolitan the city was before it became a symbol of devastation. It was a fashion capital, and both an intellectual and banking hub that gained power after the Arabian Gulf oil boom. There was a vibrant café life, and the architecture was a graceful blend of Arabic and French colonial. It was a great city to be young in.

But like most major centres there was an entrenched social hierarchy and, as a farm kid, my father felt he would have more opportunities in Canada. So, in 1965, at the age of 21, he arrived in Edmonton, hoping to make his mark. Edmonton didn't offer the cosmopolitan life of Beirut of the '60s. While oil was in the process of re-shaping the province, the next boom would still be a few years away. The province was ruled by the staid Social Credit Party, which had been founded by an evangelical radio preacher, William "Bible Bill" Aberhart. And, of course, there was the weather; that first winter was a shock.

Still, my father felt at home almost immediately. The Muslim community was well-integrated, and he saw what they had achieved there, how prosperous they had become, how they were civic leaders. At one point, three members of Alberta's legislature could trace their roots to the tiny village of Lala, including Larry Shaben, Canada's first Muslim cabinet minister, who served in the governments of Premiers Peter Lougheed and Don Getty, and Sine Chadi, the grandson of Sine Abouchadi, who nearly became leader of the Alberta Liberal party in 1994. (Sine Chadi's brother Jake became a well-known lawyer in Edmonton and he gave me my first summer law job at his firm.) Even Premier Ralph Klein once visited Lala.

My father's first major decision upon arriving was whether he would join Uncle Jimmy in Lac La Biche or stay in Edmonton.

He decided on Edmonton and found a job at a company called ECCO Heating. He excelled there, and was promoted quickly, eleven times in twenty-seven months. This experience showed him that Canada was a place where merit was rewarded, where it didn't matter what your background was. He sensed that the values prized in the Muslim community and that had been prized back home on the farm—hard work, the importance of family— were prized here.

Within a year, there was suddenly much greater pressure on him to make money. His father, my grandfather Hassen Assaf, was diagnosed with an advanced brain tumour and given no chance of survival. He was 53-years-old at the time. He was sent home from the hospital so he could pass away in the comfort and dignity of his own home, surrounded by his family. The same day he came home he lost consciousness and was pronounced dead. That night, from the town's minaret, it was announced that Hassen Assaf had sadly passed away and would be buried the next day.

It was a welcome shock to everyone when they found Hassen conscious and walking around the next morning. He was quickly returned to hospital, where the doctors said they could try a very risky surgery. Even if he survived, they said, he would certainly lose one of his senses, though they couldn't predict which one would be lost. As fate would have it, my grandfather survived surgery and lived for another forty years, but without his eyesight. He was unable to work, and this meant that Uncle Jimmy and my father, who were halfway around the world, were now responsible for taking care of Fatima and ten children. Over the next twenty years, my father put his brother through law school in Beirut and brought the rest of his siblings to Canada.

My grandfather was a wise and gentle man who taught me a great deal about life and people. His blindness made him extremely patient and insightful. I never heard him raise his voice or say an unkind word about anyone. He certainly would have had a lot to complain or be bitter about, but he was always at peace. I still deeply miss his warmth and calmness.

My own connection to Lebanon was nurtured as a kid on those trips to see my grandparents in my family's ancestral village of Lala. Though the civil war had ravaged Beirut, the village remained an oasis of sorts. The beauty of the Bekaa Valley is almost surreal. Sitting on my grandparents' porch overlooking the valley, I could see the patchwork of farms. Being in the heart of the Mediterranean, the fields and groves provide olives, grapes, cherries, figs, apricots, pomegranates and every other fruit and vegetable you can name. As a kid who grew up with Edmonton winters, it was fascinating to see exotic things growing all around. I remember how much I enjoyed figs off the tree because they were so sweet and tender, and I would ask my parents for that "fruit with the jam in the middle."

Another thing that struck me was the resilience of the people. If something was destroyed in the morning, they would start to rebuild that afternoon. Even in the midst of war, and with no central government to provide for them, the village had electricity and phone service because private enterprise found a way. Some family would get a few massive generators and wire the town, becoming the local supplier. Another bought a satellite phone system and essentially opened phone booths for people to make calls from. Of course, my heritage made me partial to them, but they have an irrepressible *joie de vivre* and they are almost wired to always try to seek light even in the darkest times.

However, the tragedy remains that a decade after my father arrived in Canada, Beirut erupted into the bloody civil war that divided the Muslim West and the Christian East. The elegant downtown became a no-man's-land, and huge swaths of the city were reduced to rubble. In the first two years of the war, 60,000 people died and the beautiful city was utterly devastated. War raged for fifteen years, driving people out of the country, destroying towns, and turning paradise into hell.

Half a world away, however, Muslims and Christians were happily integrated in Alberta. The success of this integration by the early immigrants is captured in the wise and almost poetic advice my father received from Munir Hamdon upon arriving in Canada. Munir told my father that Canadians always say please, thank you, and stand in line, and he should never forget those words if he wanted to succeed here, in this country.

Chapter Three
What's in a Name?

ALTHOUGH MY FAMILY AND LEBANESE IMMIGRANTS had a long history in Alberta, my name, Dany Hassen Assaf, didn't convey that in Edmonton in the 1970s. When I was ten, Assaf was on the back of my hockey jersey when I got into an altercation with another player. He called me a "Paki," which threw me on a number of fronts, not least that I wasn't Pakistani. Edmonton had seen a significant amount of Pakistani immigration in a short period of time, and the reception was hostile. This player didn't know that I wasn't Pakistani, but the point was to make me feel like it wasn't my game too. It landed harder than a punch because it was intended to make me feel like I didn't belong on the ice. It denied my actual identity. This incident taught me to always be ready to defend myself at a moment's notice. I got into my share of on-ice altercations and became aware how anyone can be cast as an "other" when things get rocky.

Assaf is an ethnically Lebanese last name associated with both Muslim and Christian families. I have been told that Assaf is a Jewish name as well, and people have thought I might be Jewish. The name Hassen is the name of my grandfather, which was given to me out of long-standing Lebanese tradition where the eldest son of the eldest son is named after his grandfather. This has been a tradition for centuries, and I am a proud part of that heritage.

The name Dany didn't come from any tradition. I was named after Danny Thomas, who was one of the most famous TV personalities of the 1960s and who was of Lebanese heritage. Danny Thomas was born Amos Muzyad Yaqoob Kairouz and changed his own name so his family wouldn't know he was working in Chicago nightclubs. For eleven years (1953–64), he was the star of one of the most successful shows in television. Originally titled *Make Room for Daddy*, it eventually became *The Danny Thomas Show*. Both in his TV character (he played a nightclub entertainer) and in real life, he embodied the American Dream, especially for the Lebanese. That a kid named Amos Kairouz could get to the top of the entertainment business and become rich and famous was something.

My parents viewed his success as proof of the unbounded potential that North America provided people of our heritage. They also admired Thomas's philanthropy: he founded and supported the St. Jude Children's Research Hospital in Memphis, Tennessee. But my name had an additional twist because it is spelled with only one "n," a nod to the French influence in Beirut where my father spent his early adulthood.

I remember asking my father why he spelled my name with one "n," because it was weird in 1970s Alberta and I wanted to change it. He told me to just tell anyone who asked that my name is spelled correctly, and they were wrong. It was only when I visited Quebec, on an exchange program in my second year of university, that I met someone who shared my spelling. And it took an NHL player who shared my spelling, Dany Heatley, to legitimize my name in Canada and make all of us Danys feel like we belonged.

As these names could represent someone of any three major faiths, it also perhaps shaped how people interacted with me, and why I have always been able to see myself in others. Names tap into the tribal nature of humanity, whether someone is likely to be your ally or a potential threat. But in Canada, who is our tribe? The survivors in this twenty-first century economy will be those with the broadest, most diversified networks. Names may signify origins, but they no longer signify destinations.

*

A common Canadian destination remains the hockey rink, and this rink was somewhere in suburban Edmonton. We were winning, skating hard to maintain our lead in a semi-final tournament game. I was twelve. A blur in the corner, then the collision. I felt the heat, though not the pain, of a sharp skate blade making a long scalpel-like cut deep into my thigh. The next thing I remember was the bright white hospital emergency room lights and looking at each stitch being made in my left thigh. I was watching like I had stepped out of my body. The doctor had trouble joining the cut to stitch my skin together. I told him I needed to play in the finals the next day, that it was the most important thing in the world.

"I can maybe wrap his leg more tightly so he can play," he said to my parents, looking for approval. It took thirteen stitches to close the cut. I wondered whether they would hold when I skated. I still can't recall any physical pain, but my heart was breaking at the prospect of missing the finals. I ate, drank, and slept hockey, and that last game was like the Stanley Cup final for me. The doctor methodically wrapped my thigh very tightly with extra bandages to hold the stitches in place and gave me his blessing to play. I don't think he was entirely comfortable with the idea, but in a uniquely Canadian way, he understood.

In my mind, it was an epic game. It was rough, and I wasn't a big player and took my share of hits. The action was back and forth. We scored, they scored. Having been given the chance to play, I didn't want to squander it. I managed to get two goals, but after all that effort, the game was tied 3–3 at the end of regulation time and we went to sudden death overtime. I prayed for a win. It would be humiliating to lose now.

There is a level of exhaustion that comes in overtime. You've left everything on the ice during what you hoped would be the final period, and now you have to find some hidden reserves. This makes you even hungrier to win: who wants to go through this trial only to lose? Eleven minutes into overtime, I took a pass near the red line. At some level, hockey is about creating space. A quick move, a deft pass, and in a moment the ice suddenly opens up. I was behind their centre and was able to split the tired defence and fire a hard wrist shot that found the top corner. The game was over. We won 4–3.

That game and that goal remain one of the greatest gifts fate has handed me. It provided me with a confidence and sense of possibility that shaped me forever. Other than my parents, I doubt anyone else remembers that weekend and that game. It always fascinates me how insignificant moments like this can shape a life. Moments without scripts or warning. They arrive and you move on, somehow changed, your confidence bolstered forever.

As a boy, I lived for hockey. I loved Darryl Sittler and the Toronto Maple Leafs. This was before Edmonton had an NHL team of its own, and most kids gravitated to either the Leafs or the Montreal Canadiens. When my father took me to Sport Chek that first time, I wanted everything in Leaf blue and white with the number 27. I wanted to be Darryl Sittler. The Muslim version, at least. Few things are more Canadian than hockey and what it represents, especially our creed of merit and fairness. If I suffered on the ice, it was because of my skills, not my religion. If you score, no one cares who you pray to.

Growing up, I played hockey almost every day. I logged hundreds of winter hours on the outdoor rink playing shinny. In summer, we played street hockey. I played every shift like it was an NHL tryout. I loved being part of a team. I still remember the camaraderie of the locker room and the post-game car rides home. My father reinforced the messages of teamwork, strategy, and hard work. No matter how intense the game may be, civility must prevail before and afterwards.

When I wasn't playing hockey, I was watching it, or at least trying to watch it. In those days, TV coverage was limited to CBC and CTV, with a few U.S. cable offerings, and there were no such things as PVR recordings. So we waited in unbearable anticipation each week for a televised NHL game, and there was nothing bigger than CBC's Saturday night broadcast of "Hockey Night in Canada." I literally counted the days and hours between broadcasts and I will never forget the biggest of them all, Sittler's ten-point game against the Boston Bruins in 1976. It was pure magic (his record still stands), and it demonstrated to me the possibility that every game offered.[1]

In 1979, the city of Edmonton received a gift. Our Oilers would be leaving the relative obscurity of the World Hockey League and joining the National Hockey League. And we had one of the greatest players in the world, eighteen-year-old Wayne Gretzky, although we didn't know how good he was yet. The dream of playing in the NHL became even more vivid for me and thousands of other Edmontonians with the start of the Oilers' NHL years.

*

Still, like most young hockey players, I eventually had to surrender my dream of playing in the NHL. It was time to focus on my studies in the commerce program at the University of Alberta. It found it emotionally difficult to let go of the sport and continued to play intramural hockey at university and on many beer league teams with friends.

When my wife Lisa and I had kids, I got to experience all the fun and intensity that hockey brings all over again through their games. All of my kids played, two sons (Mohamad and Zain) and two daughters (Danya and Hannah). My daughters ended up loving rowing and soccer more than hockey, but my sons stuck with the game and continued to play varsity hockey at their school, Upper Canada College. I loved watching them as much as I loved playing.

Before I had kids, people told me, "there is nothing like watching your own kid play hockey." I remember thinking that it couldn't actually be more exciting than watching professionals play. I'd seen the game where Wayne Gretzky scored his historic fiftieth goal in thirty-nine games. Only two players had ever scored fifty goals in fifty games. The first was Rocket Richard in

---

1 Years later I worked with a legal assistant who was related to Darryl Sittler, and she kindly got me a signed commemorative stick of that ten-point game. I cherish it to this day. I've had the opportunity to meet many business and political leaders from around the world, but my kids tease me that the only time they ever saw me at a loss for words is when we ran into Sittler in an elevator at the Toronto airport coming home from a family vacation. I could barely remember how to say hello.

1945, the second was Mike Bossy in the 1981/82 season. It was the gold standard for scoring. On December 30, 1981, less than a year after Bossy had hit that milestone, Gretzky was closing in on the record. He had played thirty-eight games and had forty-five goals.

My Uncle Munir, who gave my father the advice that is the title of this book, also gave us something else that turned out to be very memorable: tickets to that record-breaking game. Uncle Munir, like everyone else, wanted to see Gretzky score his historic fiftieth goal. And like everyone else, he thought it would be impossible for Gretzky to score five goals in one game. So he wasn't concerned about sharing those tickets; he assumed that he'd be able to see that historic moment at the next game, when the odds were better.

The Oilers were playing the Philadelphia Flyers that night. They were still known as the Broad Street Bullies, a tough, physical team. One thing you could rely on with the Flyers was they would get penalties, and that night was no exception. Gretzky capitalized early, getting two quick power play goals in the first period. In the second period, he completed the hat trick. In the third period, he got another goal, now only one away from the record. In the dying minutes of the game, the Oilers were clinging to a 6–5 lead, and the Flyers pulled their goalie. Gretzky fired his fiftieth into that empty net, past a diving Bill Barber. The crowd erupted, all of us thrilled to be part of that historic moment. After retiring, Gretzky said that of all his many records (sixty-one of them), that was his favourite. He also said it would be the hardest to break. I felt the same way. As far as hockey went, nothing would ever top that.

But then I had kids and saw what life can teach you.

I did enjoy watching them play more than any professional team, more than the legendary Gretzky. Sometimes I'd get so enthralled, I didn't really see the game around them. That is why I never wanted to coach them, because I knew I would be a bad coach to my own kids. I would either be too hard on them or too forgiving. It was unlikely that I'd find the right balance. I enjoyed watching them play from the stands and largely learned to keep my emotions under control to avoid being an over-the-top hockey dad. I did try to give my kids the same hockey-is-like-life lessons my father gave me on those car rides home. I loved those rides with my dad. I only hope I was able to give my kids half the guidance my father gave me in the car. It's a Canadian hockey tradition that allows the game to give us as much off the ice as on it.

I'll always remember one specific game that my son played, and thinking about it still fills my heart with joy. Mohamad was playing on the grade eight Upper Canada College team in a championship game against their archrivals, St. Michael's College. It was a great rivalry because the schools aren't far apart and many of the kids knew one another. But it was also because of St. Mike's vaunted hockey history, which included Frank Mahovlich, Dave Keon, Terrible Ted Lindsay, and dozens of other NHLers. It has the richest hockey pedigree of any school in the country. This game was on a weekday afternoon and luck would have it that I was in Toronto that week and not on one of my frequent business trips abroad. I remember the rink was filled with home team fans because St. Mike's had let the kids out early to watch the game. And what a game it was.

It was intense and tough, and after sixty minutes it was still locked at 2–2. I girded myself for an extended overtime battle. I was more nervous than I'd been for any game I'd actually played myself. In the second shift of overtime, my son Mohamad came onto the ice. He was small, a fast, intense forward, and he reminded me of myself as a player. You get tough playing hockey in northern Alberta and you learn not to let bigger players get the best of you. Mohamad played the game with the heart of a giant and I loved watching it. As the puck was dropped at the start of his shift, my mind kept wandering between two opposite scenarios: please don't make a mistake that will cause your team to lose; and please get the opportunity to win the game. The gods smiled down and my son buried the winning goal to lead UCC over St. Mike's. It was one occasion where I didn't keep my emotions contained. I think I lost my voice cheering that amazing UCC win. My hockey life came full circle in that moment as I watched my son score that epic winning goal. Gretzky's fifty goals in thirty-nine games may have been a great achievement, but it paled in comparison to my son's. Years later I would be rewarded again by seeing my younger son Zain playing on that same team and winning that same championship.

Hockey has given me so much, even without the NHL debut that I dreamed about. It taught me that, like so much in life, the journey almost always offers more than the destination. In Canada, our journeys are often travelled on a highway called hockey.

It is a game that unites us, and that's why it was so unfortunate to see Don Cherry, Canada's legendary hockey commentator and coach, use his pulpit on television's "Coach's Corner" to divide us.

On Remembrance Day, November 11, 2019, he said, "You people... love our way of life, love our milk and honey. At least you could pay a couple of bucks for poppies or something like that. These guys paid for your way of life that you enjoy in Canada."

His TV partner, Ron MacLean, tweeted, "It was a divisive moment and I am truly upset with myself for allowing it."

Sportsnet president Bart Yabsley said, "Sports brings people together, it unites us, not divides us."

Cherry was immediately fired, but he stood by his comments, and many of his fans stood by him. His influence was significant. "Don is synonymous with hockey and has played an integral role in growing the game," Yabsley said.

He did grow the game, and I even enjoyed some of his old school hockey rants over the years. When CBC still had the rights to "Hockey Night in Canada," ratings for the show would spike during "Coach's Corner." He was, at times, more popular than the game itself. But over time his perspective on the game became increasingly outdated. He didn't like finesse, or Europeans (with a few exceptions, like the battle-scarred Börje Salming). He thought Mario Lemieux was a "floater." His views were rooted in his own tough minor league career (he played one shift in the NHL), hard won, but increasingly out of the touch with how the game had evolved.

After his firing, there was a backlash from his fan base, with hashtags like #DonCherryIsRight. I was disappointed to see hockey, a game that had done so much for unity, become a wedge. It had been an integrating force in my own life, and now idea of "the other" was suddenly tied to it.

PART II
STANDING UP TO HATE

Chapter Four

Wolves at the Door

I N JANUARY 2019, MY BROTHERS WERE ONCE MORE faced with hatred, this time at the Al Rashid Mosque in Edmonton. Established in 1938, by my great-grandfather's generation, it had operated peacefully for eighty years. That peace was threatened by an Islamophobic group known as the Wolves of Odin, who came to the mosque to terrorize worshippers as they walked into Friday prayers. They were dressed like a militia, wearing uniforms and toques that said "non-believer" in Arabic. Two of them entered the mosque and were caught on security cameras. One went to the basement, the other to the top of the stairs, keeping watch. Then they went into the women's prayer area. It appeared they were conducting surveillance of the premises.

Their presence was an intrusion. After the Wolves got into arguments with some worshippers, there was the possibility that the situation could get violent and so the police were called. The Wolves told the police they were there to "debate," but it was like the Ku Klux Klan showing up in hoods to debate Christianity at a black church. The police dispersed the Wolves, but didn't charge them with anything. They had yet to commit a crime.

One of the men who'd entered the mosque said they were only there to learn more about the religion. "This is a free country," he said, "and I can question what I want." The Wolves' form of questioning was limited to intimidation and heckling as worshippers walked into the mosque. What the mosque represented to the Wolves was a concrete, visible target for their hatred and resentment.

*

Before 9/11, Islam was just another religion in the western world. After the towers fell, it became something else. Within weeks, the Al Rashid was egged, and a stone was thrown through one of the windows. Women wearing the hijab were stopped on the street and ridiculed. Muslim children were bullied at school. The mosque hired private security to keep watch at night.

Islam also became something else in the eyes of the Canadian government.

Shortly after 9/11, the Canadian Security Intelligence Service (CSIS) sent agents to Edmonton. They called members of the Al Rashid Mosque and inquired about certain Muslims. They understood that it was both the cultural and religious centre of the local Muslim population, and they attempted to recruit people of Arab descent to CSIS. They wanted to monitor the community, to insure it wasn't a hotbed of Islamic terrorism. There were no terrorists lurking in the Edmonton community, but the perception of Muslims had undergone a dramatic and almost instantaneous transformation.

The government response involved more than just CSIS. It included restrictions on immigration, restriction of rights, the rejection of religious-based mediations, and legal curbs on the use of nikabs. Essentially, it was a policy of containment. And the Al Rashid eventually found itself part of the concerted effort to face and combat these policies.

Four months before the original Al Rashid Mosque opened in 1938, there had been a Ku Klux Klan rally in Edmonton. The Klan seized on the Depression to foster hatred, to find scapegoats, and to expand their traditional base in the American South. But they didn't find many takers in Alberta. Their ranks actually diminished during the 1930s, and in 1944, they disbanded temporarily. But they rose up again in the 1960s, stronger than before, the spiritual parent to dozens of hate organizations, including the Wolves of Odin.

It was eighteen years after 9/11 that the Wolves of Odin singled out the Al Rashid Mosque as a symbol of a potentially dangerous foreign presence and began their campaign of fear by harassing and threatening worshippers. The policy of containment, ongoing media reports of Islamic terrorism, and the presidentially sanctioned and very public anti-Muslim rhetoric and policies of the United States had revived dormant fears.

The Wolves were based in Edmonton, but were a splinter group of the Soldiers of Odin, an anti-immigrant organization based in Finland. The Wolves posted a photograph posing with members of the United Conservative Party, though Premier Jason Kenney denounced the organization. They had conducted militia training outside of Lethbridge and were monitored by the RCMP. They are just one of more than 100 anti-Muslim hate groups in North America, several of whom rely on Nordic imagery for their name (Soldiers of Odin, Wolves of Vinland, Vinlanders Social Club, etc.).

It wouldn't be too much of a leap to guess that some Wolves descended from settlers who took Clifford Sifton up on his offer of 160 acres. In the early part of the twentieth century, Sifton had sent out more than a million pamphlets to the US, Europe, and the Ukraine, looking for farmers who would settle in the West. He offered 160 acres of free land and enticed them with somewhat misleading advertising ("the frontier of Manitoba is about the same latitude as Paris"). The pamphlets spoke of "building Jerusalem in this pleasant land," and pointed out that they would be free of the class restraints and prejudices of the Old World. Their grandparents of the Wolves of Odin may have farmed this free land or raised mink or opened stores. They may have bought flour or sugar or tools from my great-grandfather. Like me, they played hockey and endured the winters and cheered for the Oilers. But now they considered us to be strangers.

Not long after their first attempt to disrupt the mosque, the Wolves contacted my brother Aumer, who was a spokesman for the Al Rashid and Khalid Tarabain the long serving current president (and a cousin of mine), wanting to hold some kind of meeting. They said they were a multicultural group and wanted to learn about Islam. My brother actually entertained the idea; maybe some kind of sincerity had alighted on the Wolves. However, their demands and conditions for the meeting became increasingly strange. Among other things, they asked my brother to sign a document protecting their identity and waiving them from any liability relating to the meeting or their attendance. The waiver was now in the name of a group called the "CLANN Canada/ Worldwide." The police investigated and issued a warning to the Wolves not to return to the mosque, but no formal charges were laid. The police promised to keep a close watch, but the damage was done.

The Wolves of Odin posted a Google Maps screenshot highlighting certain Edmonton mosques, including the Al Rashid, with the caption, "Something to chew on." They were subsequently banned by Facebook for peddling hate.

Two months later, there was the horrific massacre in Christchurch, and the worry intensified. Canada wasn't immune to the growing intolerance and hatred that was building. Hate crimes against Muslims and others have risen dramatically in the last few years.

Fifty years ago, the Klan disappeared from Edmonton while the mosque flourished; faith won out over hate. But we need to be vigilant. Hatred can lie dormant for years, then rise up without warning. When the economy weakens, pressures rise, and there are politicians who will want to pit Canadians against one another for political gain. We must be vigilant against these forces simmering and then one day overwhelming us. It can happen the way Ernest Hemingway said one goes bankrupt: gradually, then suddenly.

*

But while the Wolves of Odin may have targeted the Al Rashid Mosque out of their ignorance and hatred, this building represented something quite different to the people who worshipped there. The Al Rashid Mosque was the first mosque in Canada, only the second purpose-built mosque in North America (the first was in Cedar Rapids, Iowa, built in 1922). The Al Rashid was more than just a place of worship, it was a symbol of perseverance and faith. The 1931 census showed 10,700 people of Arab background in Canada, with 645 identifying as Muslim. Most of them were in Ontario and Quebec, but a handful were scattered across the Prairies. There were about twenty Muslim families living in Edmonton, enough that they felt they needed a mosque.

The cost of building one was estimated at $5,000, well beyond the means of these Muslim families, and beyond the means of most people, given the times. The Depression had settled onto the Prairies with a vengeance. Along with the stock market collapse, the Dust Bowl had decimated prairie farms. Parts of Alberta had turned to desert. Unemployment was rampant. It wasn't a good time to be raising money.

Nevertheless, the fundraising effort was spearheaded by Hilwi Hamdon , who had come from Lebanon at the age of seventeen and settled in Fort Chipewyan, the wife of a Lebanese fur trader (and my Uncle Munir's mother). They eventually moved to Edmonton. Hilwi had no formal education and didn't speak any English when she arrived in Canada, but she taught herself to read and write English, and she had a vibrant personality that could win anyone over. She and her Muslim friends formed partnerships, made handicrafts, held bake sales and fundraising dinners, and invited Christian and Jewish women to help them. The women approached Edmonton Mayor John Fry, who had been a guest at one of their fundraising dinners, about finding appropriate land to build on. A lot was identified near the centre of the city, and it would be available for the mosque once it was demonstrated that they could raise the money to build it.

The women appealed to businesses along Jasper Avenue, getting money from Christians and Jews as well as Muslims. Despite these efforts, they didn't have enough to build. Realizing that they wouldn't find more cash in Edmonton, Hilwi and a group of women decided to venture farther afield. The mosque board registered the Arabian Muslim Association as a charitable organization, and the women travelled across Alberta, Saskatchewan, and Manitoba, looking for donations which would be tax deductible. But tax deductions are only helpful if you're making a reasonable amount of money, and many people weren't.

They managed to raise enough money to start the building but didn't have enough to complete construction. The first contractor dug the foundation, then refused to continue without money. He was fired and a second contractor was hired, Mike Dreworth. His father was Ukrainian and his mother was Russian, and Dreworth had no religious affiliation. His parents had come for Clifford Sifton's offer of free land.

Dreworth had never seen a mosque, and his design was simple: a rectangular building with two towers that flanked the entrance and a dome on the roof. It looked like a cross between a Methodist chapel and a Russian Orthodox Church, but with minarets.

The name Al Rashid is derived from the Arabic and connotes 'following the right path.' It was articulated by Lot, who appears in both the Quran and the Bible. Lot flees the corrupt city of Sodom, decrying, "Is there not among you a single rightly-guided man?" In the Bible, it is Lot's wife who famously looks back at the burning city after being told not to do so, and she is turned into a pillar of salt as punishment for not following the right path. This may be the origin of the mosque name, although there are other possibilities, including Harun al-Rashid (ca. 763–809) who ruled the Middle East during a time of peace and great wealth, and whose name translates into the just or upright.

The mosque was finished in 1938. The Depression was still weighing heavily, and another war was approaching, but the opening day was a joyful event. People from all faiths attended. The *Edmonton Journal* reported Mayor Fry saying, "It is significant that peoples of many faiths are sitting friendly together."

The culture around the Al Rashid Mosque may have started in the village of Lala, in Lebanon, but it blended seamlessly with the social fabric of Edmonton at the time. Edmonton was a cultural mosaic made up of Cree, French, Scots, English, Metis, Ukrainian and Scandinavian people, a fact reflected by their houses of worship: a Russian Orthodox Church, a synagogue, a Ukrainian Catholic Church, and a Presbyterian church, among many others.

For decades, the Al Rashid Mosque was the centre of the Arab community in Edmonton, hosting weddings, funerals, community teas and suppers. The Arab community grew dramatically after World War II. Nearly 50,000 arrived in Canada between 1946 and 1975, and Edmonton's Arab community grew to 16,000, far too many for the small mosque. In 1946, the Al Rashid was moved from its original site to a new location near the Royal Alexandra Hospital, where it sat for three decades. But in the late 1970s, Alberta's oil boom meant expansion for almost everything, including hospitals, and the Royal Alexandra needed more space and wanted to demolish the mosque. It was also discovered that the mosque hadn't been correctly situated. According to Muslim tradition, prayers are in the direction of Mecca. Worshippers had been facing the east wall, thinking it was the shortest distance. It was pointed out that the shortest distance would be northeast, over the pole. At any rate, a bigger space was needed.

There was a more sophisticated fundraising team this time around, comprised of developers and people in real estate, including my father. They had a grasp of the market, which was fueled by oil money. In 1977, a deal was made with the city that involved a land swap: the old Royal Alexandra site for a new site at 113th Street and 127th Avenue. The following year, plans were drawn up for the mosque, and by 1980, $1 million had been raised locally.

The hope was to raise half the cost the same way they did with the original: they would first appeal to the families who would use the mosque. An ad hoc building and planning committee was formed to assess the needs of the community, headed by Ali (Alic) Awid. They were able to boost the local total to $1.5 million. This time the board wanted to include Muslims in the mosque's development and appointed Ata Hai to be the architect, as well as Moe Mansur, the engineer and project manager for the building. The construction company was Nortco Construction, led by Bill Katerenchuk, who, as fate would have it, was another Ukrainian Canadian, just like the contractor who built the original mosque.

In an echo of the Al Rashid experience, $1.5 million wasn't enough to finance the cost of building, but it was enough to start towards the estimated $3 million final price tag. The community decided to start building, believing that it would be easier to raise money once people saw the mosque going up. The board's mind-set was, "Do you believe in God? Well then, God will build it." The new building was not just larger; it was a more ambitious complex. The original had a little-mosque-on-the-prairie simplicity to it. The new mosque would have a gymnasium and multi-use spaces for weddings, parties and funerals, as well as space that could be leased to the larger community to raise funds.

No one was sure where they would find the funds to finish, but they began to build anyway, and although the bills mounted, Bill Katerenchuk stood with them. After several months, the board came to the same realization that the women in 1938 had come to: they would have to go farther afield to raise the money. An emergency funding committee was quickly formed, comprised of Salem Ganam (president of the Al Rashid), developer Mahmoud (Bill) Tarrabain, Imam Yousif Chebli, and my father Mohamed, who had served as secretary-treasurer of the mosque from 1965 to 1982. In the 1930s, the women went across the Prairies, the only place that was accessible to them. This time the board went farther, to the traditional centre of Islam, the Middle East. Before leaving on a fifteen-day fundraising tour, they first had to collectively sign lines of credit totalling $1.5 million, each pledging a minimum of $100,000, so that construction wouldn't stall in their absence.

They had skin in the game at this point, so finding that $1.5 million was critical.

They started in Saudi Arabia, which at the time was using its extraordinary oil wealth to fund mosques in the U.S. They met with King Khalid, who graciously hosted them and told them he would consider their request. They continued on to the United Arab Emirates, Kuwait, and Jordan, who all kindly hosted them and who also told them that they would consider their request. They also managed to get personal donations from some of the people they met, but had yet to finalize a deal for the majority of their funding goal.

As fate would have it, while in Jordan, Bill Tarrabain ran into an old friend who told him the one place that they could get the kind of money they needed was Libya. They immediately flew to Tripoli, where they met with Dr. Sherif of the World Islamic Call Society (WICS). Sherif did his due diligence on the original Al Rashid, and said, "For this community that planted the seed of Islam in North America, a million and a half dollars for them is not a problem." The funds were to be a gift, and the only condition was that it had to formally agreed that the property would always be used as a place of worship and could not be sold or transferred without consent. The complex would be called the Canadian Islamic Centre, and the mosque itself would retain the name Al Rashid. Libya moved so quickly that the other countries stepped back to direct their money to other projects.

The project did not end there. The heady oil boom of the 1970s had turned to bust. There was a collapse of oil prices due to a world glut, and Alberta's economy was hit hard. The community had enough money to finish the building, but Dr. Sherif and WICS also wanted to ensure the annual expenses of the mosque could be maintained. They suggested building an apartment block on two acres of land next to the mosque so that the income could be used to finance the operating costs.

Dr. Sherif agreed to put up the entire cost of construction for the apartment complex. The money would be repaid out of a share of the apartment's net income. The new Al Rashid opened its doors in 1982.

The 1980s saw oil markets collapse and hard times ahead, but the mosque survived the crash and the community still found ways to fundraise and prosper. This included another fascinating intersection of the history of Islam in North America and Edmonton, when the legendary Muhammad Ali visited the city in June 1983 for a charity boxing match against Edmonton Oiler enforcer Dave Semenko, who played alongside Oiler legends Wayne Gretzky and Paul Coffey. While in Edmonton, Ali become fascinated with the history and story of this Muslim community in the Canadian North, and he made time to help them fundraise during his trip.

Looking back on this snippet of the history of Islam in North America prior to 9/11, it is remarkable to think that Ali's story included a conscientious objection to the Vietnam War on the basis of his belief that Islam is a religion of peace. His case even went to the Supreme Court of the United States, which accepted that Ali's opposition to war was based on his sincere "beliefs [as] founded on tenets of the Muslim religion." It was reported that upon hearing the news, Ali said, "I thank the Supreme Court for recognizing the sincerity of the religious teachings that I've accepted."

Ali's journey was also an example of having belief and faith in our institutions and the justice system to sort through the heated emotions of a troubled time. Because Ali became such a revered and beloved figure over the years, it is often forgotten that back then, Ali was often much maligned and thought of as simple draft dodger. However, undeterred, he said:

"I strongly object to the fact that so many newspapers have given the American public and the world the impression that I only have two alternatives in taking this stand: either I go to jail or go to the army. There is another alternative and that alternative is justice. If justice prevails, if my Constitutional rights are upheld, I will be forced to go neither to the army nor jail. In the end I am confident that justice will come my way for the truth must eventually prevail."

In many ways, his case represented the balance and fairness of our institutions to calm passions, seek truth, and protect us all even in the heat of war. No one could imagine the detour we would take in the post-9/11 world.

After building the new mosque, there was still the issue of what to do with the old mosque, the original Al Rashid, which had closed its doors in 1982 and sat vacant for several years on its original site that had now been swapped with the city. The Muslim community felt it was a historic building, so yet another fundraising committee was formed to preserve the mosque. The city of Edmonton wanted the original mosque site in order to expand the nearby Royal Alexandra Hospital, and the government very patient while the community organized a plan to have the structure designated as a heritage building, moved to a different location, and preserved.

Taking the lead on this initiative were Karen and Evelyn Hamdon, the granddaughter and grandniece of Hilwi Hamdon, who had been the chief fundraiser for the original Al Rashid, as well as Richard Awid and his wife Soraya Hafez, and Dr. Lila Fahlman, the sister of the Salem Ganam (the president of the Al Rashid). They needed to raise $75,000 to transport the mosque to Fort Edmonton Park, which featured a rebuilt version of the 1846 fort, historic houses, and a Hudson's Bay Company trading post, among many other heritage structures. They also needed to convince Edmonton's city council that it belonged there, as a critical part of the city's history. There was some resistance. Critics argued that it wasn't really a heritage building. The *Edmonton Journal* warned that "Fort Edmonton Park could be forced to accept an historical intruder." It hadn't been an intruder when it was built, so the fact that anyone could now perceive it as one wasn't a good sign.

After three years of petitions and fundraising, including funds from the Alberta government to preserve what had now been designated a provincial heritage building, the Al Rashid Mosque was lifted onto a flatbed truck and driven in the dead of night through the streets of Edmonton to its new home in Fort Edmonton Park, alongside other emblems of the first Alberta settlers. Still more money had to be raised to restore the old Al Rashid and make it presentable, but it opened its doors as a heritage building in 1992. Today there are schools in Edmonton named after these incredible women: Hilwi Hamdon, Soraya Hafez, and Lila Fahlman.

Chapter Five
The Politics of Otherness

O N JULY 5, 2008, THE BAITUN NUR MOSQUE opened in Calgary, the largest mosque in the country, spiritual home to 2,500 Muslims. Prime Minister Stephen Harper attended the ceremony, praising the mosque as the "true face of Islam."

Mr. Harper's subsequent policies reflected a different view, as did some of his other public comments. Three years later he identified "Islamicism," as opposed to terrorism, as the major threat to Canadian security. In 2015, in parliament, he directly linked Canadian mosques with the radicalization of young people. He also took on the niqab, which not a lot of women wear, as a wedge issue and appeared to connect it more broadly to all Muslims, so that he could paint them as coming from a culture that was "anti-women." It was an insult, and betrayed the contributions of Canadian Muslim women, especially during those early days in Alberta. Then Citizenship Minister Jason Kenney introduced a policy banning anyone from covering their face during citizenship ceremonies, aimed at the niqab. The policy was challenged in court by a Mississauga woman, who won her case. The decision was appealed by the Conservatives but was upheld in Federal Court. That decision was then appealed to the Supreme Court of Canada. Despite the courts' ruling, a poll showed that a majority of Canadians were in favour of the policy. It was an overhyped political wedge issue that distracted us from more pressing problems.

In 2015, Bill C-51 was passed, a security package that disproportionately affected Muslims, with bi-partisan support in parliament and the support of the public. But in the campaign for the 2015 election, the Harper government went a step farther, announcing it would establish a police hotline where citizens could report "barbaric cultural practices." The definition of barbaric cultural practices wasn't clear, but it was viewed as license to spy on immigrants, specifically Muslims. This proved to be a step too far, provoking both angry editorials and ridicule (a blog asked if wearing socks with sandals counted as a "barbaric cultural practice").

"We need to stand up for our values," said Chris Alexander, Minister of Citizenship and Immigration. But the nature of those Canadian values was muddied by the pledge of a "barbaric practices" hotline. We already have 911, which is a well-established hotline for actual criminal and barbaric behavior, backstopped by the *Criminal Code of Canada*. Was spying on and vilifying our fellow citizens, pitting Canadians against one another for political gain—a favoured technique of East Germany's Stasi—one of our values? It was a long way from Wilfrid Laurier's cry a century earlier that Canada would become "the star towards which all men who love progress and freedom shall come." Among those who came were Muslims escaping military service in the Ottoman Empire, some of whom ended up in Alberta.

When my great-grandfather's generation was trying to raise money for the mosque in Edmonton, they appealed to everyone and received a favourable response from everyone. The idea of the outsider hadn't taken root; their commonality was greater than their differences. They had all come from somewhere to this hostile land.

That commonality has now frayed and our differences are more pronounced. And there are some who exploit the cracks in our mosaic for political advantage. It can be easier to rally a crowd against a perceived enemy than it is to do the hard work of nurturing new ideas and forging the necessary consensus to support a shared vision for the future. A century ago, every circuit preacher knew that it was God who brings them into the tent, but it is the devil that keeps them there. The world is moving faster and becoming more competitive by the day, and we don't have time to waste on false prophets and political gimmicks.

When people hate an entire group, one of the things they may be hating is the sense of belonging that the members of that group share with each other, something that the hater may not have and may envy. For others, it is easier to hate someone else's identity than to create their own. It often says more about the hater than the hated.

*

To the south of us, America is the canary in the nationalist coal mine. It has always see-sawed between the politics of hope and the politics of fear, but the Trump presidency elevated the politics of fear to new heights. Hope worked in the 1960s with a youthful, glamourous JFK telling a nation to "Ask not what your country can do for you, ask what you can do for your country." Barack Obama ran on a message of hope, telling the nation, "Hope is the belief that destiny will not be written for us, but by us, by the men and women who are not content to settle for the world as it is, who have the courage to remake the world as it should be."

George H.W. Bush had his "thousand points of light," and a kinder, gentler nation. Ronald Reagan spoke of "morning in America." Trump's response to anti-racism protesters, who filled the streets in the wake of the death of George Floyd at the hands of a Minneapolis police officer, was: "When the looting starts, the shooting starts." No politician since Joseph McCarthy in the 1950s exploited the fears and insecurities of the electorate to such advantage. A group of political scientists rated Trump the most polarizing president in history by a wide margin.

In the summer of 2019, Trump addressed four Democratic Congresswomen of colour in a series of tweets. "So interesting to see 'Progressive' Democrat Congresswomen, who originally came from countries whose governments are a complete and total catastrophe, the worst, most corrupt and inept anywhere in the world (if they even have a functioning government at all), now loudly and viciously telling the people of the United States, the greatest and most powerful nation on earth, how our government is to be run."

Three of the Congresswomen he was referring to, Alexandria Ocasio-Cortez, Rashida Tlaib and Ayanna Pressley, were born in the U.S., which, many argued at the time, did have an inept government that was "a complete and total catastrophe." The fourth, Ilhan Omar, was a Somalian refugee. Both Omar and Tlaib were Muslim. "Why don't they go back and help fix the totally broken and crime infested places from which they came... you can't leave fast enough."

Ocasio-Cortez tweeted in response, "Mr. President, the country I 'come from,' and the country we all swear to, is the United States. But given how you've destroyed our order with inhumane camps, all at a benefit to you and the corps who profit off them, you are absolutely right about the corruption laid at your feet."

After Trump's flurry of tweets, the *New York Times* asked its readers if they had ever been told to "go back." It received 16,000 responses. "Many recalled first becoming aware of their 'otherness' as young children," the *Times* article read, "and said that slurs have followed them into adulthood. Their stories span decades, with notable upticks after 9/11 and Mr. Trump's election."

One of the stories was from a Muslim woman who was born and raised in Texas. She was thirteen when she was first told to go home. "It was," she said, "the first time I felt someone's hatred of me so viscerally. I felt confused, scared, angry and alone. He was the first of many—usually men, usually white, usually angry—who have yelled at me to go home... No matter how many American flags I put on my lawn, how diligently I pursue the American dream that my parents came here for or how hard I try to be the model citizen, it seems I am the perennial 'other.'"

Thousands of stories echoed this sentiment. A Los Angeles man named Keian Razipour said, "I've been called a terrorist and Osama bin Laden's son. I've been told to go on my jihad. I've been called a member of al-Qaeda and the Taliban. These all came during high school. I was born here, yet others told me I didn't belong."

Several responses were from people who had told others to "go back" and now regretted it. An Omaha man said, "Unfortunately, I do not want to admit this, but I have told people, people who are Americans, to go back to their country (which does not make much sense other than the fact that they look different from the majority) and I feel horrible for it. While I do regret these actions, I felt emboldened at the time because of the current political climate."

The politics of hate allows and sometimes encourages hatred among certain elements of the population. It can legitimize their hate. In his book, *Overcoming Destructive Anger*, psychologist Bernard Golden wrote, "Acts of hate are attempts to distract one-self from feelings such as helplessness, powerlessness, injustice, inadequacy and shame. Hate is grounded in some sense of perceived threat."

It can be politically useful to have an enemy. Trump had many, both real and perceived, including the media, liberals, Obama, his own cabinet, etc. Some enemies become friends then enemies again (North Korea, Russia). But he was steadfast in his antipathy toward Muslims. It was evident in his 2016 campaign. He recognized the undercurrent of fear, the residue of 9/11 in parts of the electorate, and tapped into it, in part by selling Americans on the idea they were the victims. "Islam hates us," Trump proclaimed. Though in the course of his term, he was selective in his Islamophobia (Pakistan was "nothing but lies and deceit," while Saudi Arabia remained a staunch ally despite the suspected sanctioned murder of a *Washington Post* journalist). He announced that Syrian refugees, predominantly women and children, could be agents of ISIS, "a 200,000-man army, maybe."

During the 2016 campaign, Trump called for "a total and complete shut-down" of Muslims coming into the United States. Seven days after becoming president in January 2017, he issued an Executive Order titled "Protecting the Nation from Foreign Terrorist Entry into the United States." Colloquially, it was known as "the Muslim ban," and it banned immigrants from Iran, Iraq, Sudan, Syria, Libya, Yemen, and Somalia. His position was challenged in court, but ultimately upheld up by the Supreme Court. Public opinion moved toward Trump's view: 47 percent of Americans supported his visa restrictions, and a majority wanted mosques to be under surveillance.

The numbers didn't support this fear and antagonism. During a fifteen-year period, an average of twenty-eight Muslims in the

U.S. were associated with violent extremism annually, and most of those acts were in the form of going abroad to join radical movements. This from a population of 3.5 million Muslims. To put it in perspective, in 2017, Muslim extremists killed seventeen people in the U.S., while 267 Americans were killed in mass shootings by white men.

The U.S. sees more acts of violence initiated by white supremacists than by Muslims. The Center for Investigative Reporting examined 201 terrorist incidents on U.S. soil between 2008 and 2016 and noted that right-wing extremists were responsible for 115 (this included white supremacists, militias, and "sovereign citizens"), compared to 63 cases by Islamist extremists. In October 2020, a plot involving fanatic right-wing militiamen was uncovered in Michigan. They planned to kidnap the governor, put her on trial for treason, and then execute her in the hopes of instigating a civil war.

The actions of the Unite the Right rally at Charlottesville, Virginia, where protestors chanted racist and Nazi slogans, resulted in the death of a counter-protester named Heather Heyer and injuries to nineteen others. Afterward, Trump said there were "very fine people on both sides." By equating the two, Trump effectively sanctioned the white supremacists, something he would continue to do, sometimes subtly, sometimes overtly.

In 2018, there were 100 anti-Muslim hate groups in the U.S. They depict Muslims as violent and intolerant, and some endorse the conspiracy theory that the objective of American Muslims is to overthrow democracy and replace it with Islamic despotism, known as "civilization jihad," which will replace the constitution with Sharia law.

Democracy actually was under credible assault, though not from jihadists. The threat was from the President himself. In June 2020, he sent the military to disperse a peaceful crowd of anti-racism protesters outside the White House. They used noxious gas and rubber bullets to create a corridor so Trump could walk the few blocks to St. John's Episcopal Church for a photo op where he held up a Bible. His actions were condemned by both religious leaders and by the military. Several former generals, including James Mattis, spoke out against using the military against

America's own citizens. Mattis, a former Defense Secretary under Trump and a U.S. Marine general whose nickname had been "Mad Dog," wrote, "I have watched this week's unfolding events, angry and appalled... Donald Trump is the first president in my lifetime who does not even try and unite the American people—does not even pretend to try."

To justify his actions, Trump took a familiar tack: radicalize the protestors. He announced in a tweet that the crowd was made up of "professional anarchists, violent mobs, arsonists, looters, criminals, rioters, Antifa and others." He went on to say that "state and local governments have failed to take necessary action to safeguard their residents," and that he was the "President of law and order."

The institutionalizing of hatred is a dangerous, although effective, strategy. When Trump appointed Stephen Miller, who has openly endorsed white supremacist views, to determine immigration policy (and write some of Trump's more toxic speeches), it was a clear signal as to where the administration stood on race. Twenty-seven senators signed a letter demanding that Miller be fired, that his interests weren't in national security but in white supremacy.

It was into this atmosphere that a Nashville newspaper, *The Tennessean*, allowed a full-page ad to appear that said Islam was going to detonate a nuclear bomb in the city. The ad even named the date. The ad should have been disallowed simply on legal grounds: inciting the evacuation of a city. It also should have been disallowed on moral grounds, and certainly under the umbrella of hate speech. The ad was placed by a group called Ministry of Future for America, which had a stated mission to "proclaim the final warning message" from the Bible.

The Islamic nuclear reckoning came and went without incident, but the fallout from the ad, placed in the state's largest newspaper, lingered.

*

At its most fundamental level, racist policies are sold as a way of keeping the country safe; the borders are closed to "Muslim terrorists" and "Mexican rapists." In reality, these policies make the country a more dangerous place. One of the reasons for this is that by essentially sanctioning white nationalism, the rise in hate groups only takes up more of the FBI's time and resources, with increased concerns about domestic terrorism. It foments the kind of anger and disillusionment that can breed terrorism, and just further divides the home front.

In August 2020, former Homeland Security Official Elizabeth Neumann was asked in an interview to what extent the Trump administration's policies were being shaped by white nationalist ideology. "I was deeply disappointed in what I saw," she said. "And I came to realize that there is some design to it... I do think there are people who hold a white nationalist viewpoint, and that that is actually impacting these policies." Neumann and more than seventy other former officials went public with concerns that the Trump administration had "imperilled" national security, and that Trump was "dangerously unfit" for the job. "We started to see the rise of the white supremacist agenda," she said. "I do think the president's divisive language is indirectly tied to some of the attacks that we have seen in the last two years... We are less safe today because of his leadership. We will continue to be less safe as long as he is in control."

By creating threats, or inflating the danger posed by any group, the result is, ironically, a country that is less safe. Since 9/11, America has engaged in a misguided war with Iraq and stoked division by targeting Muslims at home. It sure hasn't made Americans stronger or wealthier. One of Osama bin Laden's goals was to goad the US into quagmires, which could drain its military and economic resources just as he had seen happen with the Soviets in Afghanistan. The net effect of the Iraq war was to hand the country over to the regime in Iran. It still strikes me as ironic that the key architect of the war in Iraq was Dick Cheney, an avid fly fisher, who bit down hardest on the bait that bin Laden cast out there. It reminds me of one of Napoleon's most famous quotes, "Never interrupt your enemy when he is making a mistake."

This vortex of tension, scapegoating, economic pressure, racism, and lack of trust in government were fomented by Trump's demagogic leadership and his unfiltered access to the 88 million people that followed his Twitter account. These issues were intensified by the raging Coronavirus pandemic, and culminated in the traumatizing assault and attempted insurrection that took place on Capitol Hill on January 6, 2021. Trump incited the crowd, telling them, in what will become the historic words of a sitting President, to march and take back their country. He instructed them: "You'll never take back our country with weakness. You have to show strength. You have to be strong."

It was the biggest attack on Washington since 1812 and, if not for a handful of leaders who finally stepped off the Trump train at virtually the last minute, who knows what could have been. It doesn't take a wild imagination to picture the ensuing chaos and violence that would have transpired if the Vice President had entertained the idea of some contrived ploy to have a fourteen-day "Commission" investigate made-up voter fraud allegations and send the election results back to the states to "recertify." This could have spelled the end of American democracy as we know it. Just think if one of those senators pushing to overturn the election was sitting in the chair of Vice President on January 6, 2021. As Trump himself told the crowd that day: "All Vice President Pence has to do is send it back to the states to recertify, and we become President, and you are the happiest people."

If that happened, what would history be writing now? Even more ominous, the two leading senators pushing the "stolen" election claims are eyeing the Presidency in 2024.

It was also horrifying to realize that the Capitol Hill insurrectionist leaders were hoping to capture and kill the Vice President and Speaker of the House. They sported army fatigues, carried weapons and zip ties, and openly claimed that the only remedy to their "concerns" was death to those leaders. It required the deployment of 25,000 National Guard troops, who themselves had to be vetted to ensure that none of them supported white supremacist ideologies, to fortify the subsequent inauguration of President Biden (a deployment larger than the U.S. had in Iraq and Afghanistan combined at the time). In the twenty years since 9/11, we have come full circle; there now appear to be versions of a "white ISIS" emerging in the United States. The cancer of extremism threatens to consume us all.

Throughout history, societies have looked for scapegoats when times get tough. They claim that things will only get better if we get rid of x, y, or z. It isn't hard for this to become a large-scale delusion. In a free society, everyone's place is protected or no one is. To paraphrase the familiar words of Martin Niemöller, a Lutheran Pastor and opponent of the Nazi regime: first they came for those people and I did not speak out, because I was not one of those people. Then they came for the others and I did not speak out, because I was not one of the others. Then they came for me and there was no one left to speak for me.

There are many reasons why we hate. One is because we fear things that are different from us. Behavioural researcher Patrick Wanis notes that when we feel threatened by those we perceive as outsiders, we turn toward those we identify with as a survival mechanism. But today our survival as a civilization depends on embracing those we perceive as outsiders and expanding our definition of what it means to belong to a tribe. In our unprecedented era, which is so deeply built on technological growth, economic success will come to those whose reach extends furthest.

Chapter Six

Seeing and Being Seen

THE 1992 DISNEY FILM *ALADDIN,* a film intended for nine-year-olds, featured a theme song with lyrics that said Aladdin came from "a faraway place, where the caravan camels roam, where they cut off your ear if they don't like your face. It's barbaric, but hey, it's home." It was immediately criticized by Arab-American groups for perpetuating a racial stereotype, and the lyrics were changed for the video version. Two years later, *True Lies,* starring Arnold Schwarzenegger, featured a terrorist group named "the Crimson Jihad," prompting protests in New York and Los Angeles by Arab-American advocacy groups. There were caricatures of Arab terrorists and a general conflating of Arab and Muslim in the film.

Of course, it is unlikely that 1.8 billion people who are members of a faith that has endured for almost 1500 years are all dark and evil. Market forces would suggest it has had too many adherents for far too long not to offer something beautiful to its believers. Like the other major faiths, Islam offers comfort and light. They are looking for something positive, which is one reason why it's one of the world's fastest-growing religions. But you might not know that from its portrayal in popular culture. There seems to be an obsession with exclusively focusing on the criminals and bad apples. Sadly, history has shown that Islam is not the only faith infected with a small number of radicals and violent extremists—no religion has a monopoly on that.

One critic noted that in film and television, Arabs tend to fall into three different stereotypes: belly dancers, billionaires, and bombers. This goes back to the beginning of film history. The short that Thomas Edison used in 1897 to apply for a patent for his Kinetoscope featured an Arab belly dancer. More recently, Arabs have been the bad guys. At the movies, as in politics, narratives tend to require perceived villains: Indigenous peoples in old Western films, Nazis in World War II films, and Russians in Cold War films. Arabs are now one of the go-to enemies.

In his book *The TV Arab*, Jack Shaheen documented more than twenty major films between 1975 and 1984 that featured Arab villains, including *Iron Eagle*, *Navy SEALs*, *Delta Force 3*, and many others. Shaheen listed more than 100 films and TV shows with negative depictions. In the thirty-five years since, and especially post-9/11, the stakes have been raised considerably higher. Stereotypes, scapegoating, and generalizations have exploded. Some movies, such as *The Siege*, make direct onscreen links between Muslim rituals and terrorist violence.

I have sometimes heard tropes like "not all Muslims are terrorists, but all terrorism involves Muslims." There are few things more offensive to me than ignorant statements like that. No one says, "not all Europeans wish for world war, but every world war involves Europeans."

We don't see a lot of Arab villains in Canadian films because, for the most part, we don't see a lot of Canadian films (the villain here is usually the box office). But American films are seen around the world. A report by the Islamic Human Rights Commission argued that Hollywood had a crucial role in how the general public viewed Muslims and that the depictions were unfavourable. It is basic logic that it is easier to mistreat people who have been dehumanized for us. No one wants to see a movie villain go unscathed, and this translates into how people are perceived in real life. These stereotypes become entrenched because they are in fact seen by millions of people, sometimes in hundreds of countries, and on many platforms. It used to be that a film played for a few weeks in the local cinema then disappeared, often fading away from our imaginations as well. Now, with digital movie channels, nothing ever really goes away. The record is permanent and recycled over and over again.

In Britain, a survey of Muslims noted that many of them felt that negative portrayals in film and TV had real consequences on their lives, finding "a direct correlation between media portrayal and their social experience of exclusion, hatred, discrimination and violence." The problem, the study found, wasn't just that there were negative images of Muslims in film; it was that these were the *only* images. There has been little or no effort to provide balance in the portrayals.

Hollywood is no longer the creative force it once was. It generally goes with what works (eleven X-Men movies, eight Batman movies, and six Spider-Man movies). And, sadly, what works in the current climate are Muslim villains.

*

It is hard for reality to compete with movies and television. This is especially true when that reality doesn't offer a better example. In 2009, Firouzeh Zarabi-Majd, a young Muslim of Iranian descent, became a Toronto police officer. She was stationed at 51 Division, which is directly south of where I live. That area of Toronto has a very diverse population, including many immigrants trying to find belonging in society. Toronto is a city that has 51 percent visible minorities and a police force that is 75 percent white. The gap at 51 Division was even wider; there were few female or Muslim officers. With Zarabi-Majd, more locals who lived in that Division would see someone who looked like them in a police uniform, which is a distinct advantage with community policing.

But in 2018, after almost a decade as a police officer, Zarabi-Majd filed a claim with Ontario's Human Rights Tribunal where she alleged "demeaning, sexist, racist and Islamophobic comments" as well as ongoing sexual harassment. She stated that the police culture was one in which "misogyny and racism are normalized." The majority of police officers are not racist or misogynists, but a few influential voices can unfortunately shape cultures within organizations by creating or condoning certain behaviors.

Zarabi-Majd was asked if she was "a Musi" (a derogatory reference to Muslims) by one superior officer, a name that stuck. Some other officers called her that behind her back, then eventually to her face. Zarabi-Majd was initially afraid to come forward with allegations against fellow officers, fearful for her safety. She worried that when she called for back-up, there wouldn't be any. Or maybe officers would just respond slowly. She said that she'd seen it happen with unpopular cops.

She also claimed that racialized officers were victims of biased promotional practices and given fewer opportunities for professional development. In the end, she was diagnosed with Post-Traumatic Stress Disorder, and left the force.

It is disheartening that in my own backyard, there is Islamophobia that prevents fellow Canadians from making a full contribution to our society and from being judged on their merits. There are few things that strike me as more un-Canadian than that. Even more upsetting is that in an area of the city that could most benefit from a diverse police presence, an opportunity was squandered. What Muslim woman will want to sign up for the police force in the wake of Zarabi-Majd's allegations? It raises a disturbing question for the community: if this is how a Muslim policewoman was treated by her own, how would the police force treat the Muslim women they have sworn to serve and protect?

Regrettably, Firouzeh Zarabi-Majd's case wasn't unique. In 2017, five members of the Canadian Security Intelligence Service (CSIS) filed a $35 million lawsuit against their employer, alleging Islamophobic, sexist, and racist treatment. Three of the complainants were Muslim. One was a Muslim analyst who had been with the agency for twenty years and alleged he was called "a sand monkey" by his boss. Another was a female Muslim officer who had been with CSIS for a decade. She said her hijab aroused suspicion. She was told to report on all activities within the Muslim community, and also that her security clearance could be revoked for associating with Muslims, which was "perceived as antithetical to CSIS." She was denied access to certain source files because she was Muslim. Yet another complainant was a gay man with a Muslim partner. He was told by his manager, "Careful your Muslim in-laws don't behead you in your sleep for being homo."

There is an obvious irony here. Ultimately, this is behavior that weakens rather than strengthens our national security. CSIS has identified ISIS as a major threat, and ISIS's *Dabiq* magazine has reprinted calls to violent action. In October 2014, Canadian-born ISIS supporter Martin Couture-Rouleau rammed a car into a group of Canadian soldiers at a shopping center in Quebec, killing one soldier and wounding another. Shouldn't CSIS have viewed the employment of multilingual Muslim employees as invaluable? Instead, these employees were marginalized, harassed, and mistrusted. One manager was heard to say that "Muslim women were inferior" and also that Barack Obama was "a member of the Muslim Brotherhood." This should be cause for alarm given that it was coming from our most sophisticated spy agency.

"The culture of CSIS is hostile to Muslims, and this is more than just an unfriendly work environment," said a Muslim employee with twenty years at CSIS. "It is deeply ingrained prejudice and distrust for Muslims which has meant that Muslims are used and managed as needed, but are not part of the team." At a social event, a manager emphatically stated, "All Muslims are terrorists." That kind of talk is not only offensive but an insult to the professionalism of the majority of CSIS personnel.

This should be one of the levels on which our multicultural society works best: having members who are familiar with foreign customs and nuances, and who speak foreign languages. Instead, minorities are considered outsiders or even enemies. What happens when a group of people becomes marginalized, when it loses faith in police protection, when it doesn't see itself among those who serve and protect? One response is that some will decide to take matters into their own hands.

That's what happened in 2018, when a sinister campaign appeared online in England. "Punish a Muslim Day" offered points for different punishments, from pulling off a woman's headscarf to bombing a mosque. The campaign put police on alert as far away as New York, where they expanded patrols around mosques. In the New York borough of Brooklyn, a group of Muslims felt this wasn't enough. They formed a Muslim version of Neighbourhood Watch, with thirty members of an all-volunteer group called the Muslim Community Patrol & Services. They had uniforms and perfunctory training from off-duty police officers, and two patrol cars that were painted to look like police cars.

There was an immediate backlash, although the Muslim force wasn't the first local civilian force to operate in Brooklyn: the Hassidic neighbourhoods had the Shomrim, and the Brooklyn Asian Safety Patrol worked in Sunset Park. The unarmed Muslim force offered translation services and offered help with cultural differences. They had the support of at least one commanding officer in Brooklyn, as well as the borough president, who said: "More than buildings went down in 9/11. Trust between communities went down. We are building it back one brick at a time, and this patrol is one of those bricks."

A Canadian website, Rebel Media, suggested the group was essentially the first step in establishing Shariah law in America. Far right conspiracy theorists jumped onto the bandwagon. They failed to realize that there are critical areas where the population needs to see itself represented and policing is one of them. This is yet another case of what happens when we retreat into tribalism. We become weaker as a society. Unity results in strength, which leads to prosperity. In the case of policing, tribalism isn't just counter-productive, it's dangerous.

The wake-up call for more diverse and inclusive policing came not from Firouzeh Zarabi-Majd's case, or similar complaints from female or racialized officers in Toronto, but from an incident that happened 1,100 kilometres away.

When George Floyd was cruelly killed in slow motion before our eyes by a Minneapolis police officer, his death captured on camera, it sparked global outrage. Murals appeared on walls in Brussels and Kenya and Syria. People marched and protested in dozens of countries. Floyd's last words, "I can't breathe," became a rallying cry. In Toronto, there were marches and calls for police reform. The Toronto police noted that they had made great progress: they went from 10 percent visible minority officers in 2000 to 24 percent in 2020. It's not enough, but it's a start.

We can't go back and rectify every past wrong and negative portrayal, but free societies must continuously seek greater justice and fairness. The further we stray from these touchstones, the more our way of life is jeopardized and our society is out of balance. The most enduring structures, whether in architecture, nature, or human relationships, are those in balance.

These times require that we move away from thinking in terms of "my story" and instead renew and reaffirm the collective idea of "our story." Building the future does not require destroying our past, just ensuring we all do our part to improve and build on it.

PART III
THE CANADIAN WAY

Chapter Seven
A Country of Immigrants

C ANADA'S IMPERFECT AND OFTEN BLOODY origin story includes the cold reality of colonialism and the rivalry of the great powers of the time, England and France. That rivalry culminated in the battle on the Plains of Abraham in 1759, with an insecure General Wolfe besting the reluctant French commander Montcalm. France surrendered Canada to the British, leaving thousands of French-speaking immigrants under British rule. Often the outcome of war involves the subjugation of the conquered. In the case of the French, this would have meant forced religious conversions and losing all traces of their language and culture. But not this time. Francophones retained their language, religion, and customs. By the time of Canada's founding on July 1, 1867, our constitution, known then as the *British North America Act*, guaranteed the "rights and privileges" of both Protestants and Catholics and enshrined bilingualism. The seeds of accommodation had been planted.

The accommodation of the Indigenous population, unfortunately, took a much different and ultimately tragic course. John A. Macdonald, our first prime minister and father of confederation, wanted to avoid the bloody wars that America was experiencing with its Indigenous peoples. He preferred a policy of appeasement, but this appeasement was limited. Macdonald was a political pragmatist, and when the plains natives were starving because their traditional source of food, the buffalo, had been all but wiped out, he recommended sending food "to where the tomahawks are sharpest." That is, to appease the strongest tribes while others starved. The policies of containment, the eradication of tribal customs and languages, the predatory treaties, all left a wound that has yet to heal 150 years later.

Canada has always been an argument with itself: French/English; East/West; federal/provincial; Leafs/Canadiens/Oilers. But it has been, for the most part, a civilized argument. And although we have had tragic episodes with our Indigenous peoples, we have been much better as far as immigration goes. Perhaps that is because we are all immigrants, with our hardwired human curiosity to explore and enjoy the marvels of our wonderful planet. It is said that even the Indigenous peoples came to Canada across the Bering Isthmus, albeit 15,000 years ago. In the end, by virtue of our humanity, we are reminded that we all occupy a small role as trustees of this planet and we have a responsibility to treat it and all its inhabitants with respect wherever we find ourselves in every era.

In the early part of the twentieth century, when Clifford Sifton was trying to populate the plains, he first wanted immigrants from Scandinavia, Germany, England, and the United States. When these numbers weren't enough, he realized he would have to expand his search to Ukrainians, Russians, Poles and others. The "men in the sheepskin coats," as they were called, were responsible for cultivating millions of acres of farmland, creating the agricultural economy that is now a large part of our modern economy. Early on, Canada understood the need for immigrants and the benefits that came with them.

For the most part, we have been generous in terms of the numbers we allow. In 2020, the federal government set a target of 341,000, a little less than 1 percent of the existing population. According to Statistics Canada, 21.9 percent of the population is already comprised of immigrants, the highest percentage in the developed world. Almost as important as the number of immigrants is the attitude toward immigrants. An Environics poll found that only a third of Canadians felt there was too much immigration to Canada. And eight out of ten Canadians felt that immigration helped the economy.

When COVID-19 hit, borders all around the world closed, effectively halting immigration. But even before the borders closed, many other countries had already begun restricting immigration. One of the war cries of populist governments is to reclaim the country from the perceived influence of immigrants.

One of the uncomfortable truths seldom faced by anti-immigration populist governments is that, while they may not want immigrants, they need them.

Hungarian Prime Minister Viktor Orbán is one of the most vocal European Union anti-immigrant leaders. He refers to immigrants as "invaders" and has put up barbed wire fences to keep out refugees. He has denied food to those in detention centres. There is an irony to Orbán's words because the world had at one time offered refuge to many Hungarians who fled the oppressive communist regime in 1956. The Hungarian media is largely controlled by Orbán, and every day there are news stories that reinforce the need to protect the borders from foreigners. Orbán has given speeches championing "ethnic homogeneity" as a way to boost the economy and to keep the economy safe.

"Ethnic homogeneity" does neither of these things, as Orbán knows. While maintaining a virulent public anti-immigrant stance, Hungary has very quietly opened the back door to let in immigrants. In 2018, there were 49,500 work permits held by non-EU citizens in Hungary, up from only 7,300 in 2016. Orbán and other anti-immigrant leaders are faced with the stark realities of the twenty-first century economy and the increased mobility of populations. People in eastern Europe migrate to western Europe, which is wealthier. So eastern European countries like Hungary and Poland have to recruit workers from somewhere or face severe economic consequences. South Korea delayed opening a $295 million tire factory in Hungary because of problems with recruiting workers.

President Donald Trump faced a similar problem with his own anti-immigration policy. Leaders from Silicon Valley lobbied the Trump administration to let in immigrants or risk diluting the talent pool and becoming less competitive globally. Immigrants represent about 25 percent of U.S. inventors and entrepreneurs, and half of the founders of start-up unicorns. Germany, which welcomed large numbers of Syrian refugees, has similar statistics; immigrants founded more than 25 percent of German start-ups, and the most growth-oriented and innovative ventures. The Silicon Valley Leadership Group said 58 out of 100 engineers in Silicon Valley's innovation economy were born outside the U.S. "For us not to be celebrating that and to be intentionally blocking that is a sad day for this country," said Carl Guardino, head of the group. He also noted that "reducing skilled immigrants both makes our companies less competitive and increases the likelihood that if the right skills can't be found locally, their jobs will move to countries such as Canada that actively welcome educated immigrants."

In the United Kingdom, Brexit was partly a vote against immigration. While every developed country was hit hard economically during the pandemic, the U.K. recorded its most dramatic recession in 300 years. It faced the dual threat of fewer immigrants and the quiet exodus of highly educated Britons who left for Europe.

The benefits of immigrants have never been greater. The arguments in favour of relatively high immigration levels have chiefly been economic. Immigrants tend to be entrepreneurial and produce a net gain for any national economy. The immediate economic benefits are easily measurable. What is more difficult to measure is the advantage to having a multicultural population, like Canada, that is equipped to deal with almost any other culture or nation on earth.

*

There is yet another argument in favour of immigration, existential rather than economic. Canada, like most developed countries, has an aging population and declining birth rates. In 2015, one Canadian in six was over the age of 65. By 2030 it will be one in four. Canada's fertility rate is 1.5 births per family, less than the 2.1 necessary just to keep the population at its existing level. We are also living longer. This means there will be fewer young people to pay for aging seniors who are taxing both the health care and pension systems. We have seen what happens in countries like Japan, which has traditionally had one of the lowest immigration levels in the developed world (fewer than 1.75 percent of the country are immigrants, compared to Canada's almost 22 percent). Japan also has an exceptionally aged population. These are among the factors contributing to the country's economic stagnation, which has lasted for decades.

These demographic trends were looming before the COVID-19 pandemic arrived and changed the landscape. The coronavirus sparked many changes in behavior. One thing it was expected to do was produce a miniature baby boom. Everyone was home all the time. It made sense. Except the opposite happened. The economic uncertainty of the virus meant that many young couples put off further investments in parenthood. The Brookings Institution in Washington predicted that the pandemic would result in 500,000 fewer American births. The dropping fertility rate is expected to continue far past the pandemic.

A study commissioned by the Bill and Melinda Gates Foundation and published in *The Lancet* predicted that the global fertility rate will be 1.66 by the end of the century. Twenty-three countries will lose more than half their population. China would lose 48.18 percent, Russia 27.18 percent, Brazil 22.22 percent. Canada, however, is an outlier. It is predicted to gain 22.54 percent of its population by the end of the century.

Hungary is among the countries expected to lose half their population. One of Prime Minister Orbán's responses to this looming disaster has been to try and bribe Hungarians into having more children. The government offered loans that didn't have to be repaid if couples had at least three children. Those who had four got a lifetime exemption from paying income tax. There are problems with his model, however. Not the least of which is believing the decision to bring children into the world is something you can simply bribe people into doing. And what happens if those four children grow up and see there is more opportunity in Paris, Berlin, New York, or Dubai, and decide to leave?

Orbán continues to publicly maintain a virulent anti-immigrant stance ("migration for us is surrender," he says). One wonders what would happen if his idea of national grandeur was market tested with his own people. Or if Canada opened its borders and somehow had a "sale" on immigration for Hungarians? The likely result would be that people would care more about economic opportunity than nationalism and vote with their feet, abandoning Orbán.

*

We seem to have become defensive, and our perspective is getting smaller rather than expanding to serve the needs of the times. Immigration has become a major wedge issue. Citizens in the United States and the United Kingdom prospered from the work of generations of immigrants seeking a new life, but now there is a disturbing sentiment that immigrants have somehow stolen something from them. Sometimes it's slightly intangible, a sense of home, a way of life. Sometimes it is more tangible: jobs.

Prior to the 2016 election, when Trump supporters talked about losing a "way of life," it wasn't always clear what they meant. For people in the Rust Belt, it was a time when there was something approaching full employment, when factories were operating, before jobs were exported to cheaper labour markets offshore. The jobs went to other countries, and now other countries were sending their people to the U.S. to take what jobs were left. This is the simplistic though effective message that populist politicians and false prophets often peddle when they don't have real answers and solutions. But we can't recover the past. We have to look to the future.

In the midst of the COVID-19 crisis, the *Globe and Mail* ran an editorial that reprinted the old joke: How do you get fifty Canadians out of a swimming pool? Ask them to please get out of the swimming pool. It would be a lot more costly and disruptive if we had to hire police officers to get fifty people out of a pool at closing time. Our general faith in authority is sometimes derided by our American neighbours, and it's true we lack their appetite for risk-taking, which has cost us some on the innovation front. However, there are advantages to peace, order, and good government (and to saying "please and thank you" and standing in line).

One of them is a faith in government. When the pandemic landed, we wore the masks, washed our hands, stayed two metres apart as instructed. As a result, our infections were a fraction of what the U.S. experienced. Given the population ratio of roughly ten-to-one, the U.S. should have had roughly ten times as many cases. Unfortunately, they had almost *forty times* the number. The result in both countries reflected the will and behavior of the people.

The unbridled will of the people can be a double-edged sword, and that's why courts serve as our stoic stabilizers. In 2016, when Trump was elected, many analysts viewed it as a vote against the establishment, one that had lost the trust of, and largely failed, the middle class and what was left of the working class. Trump was a way to disrupt the system. After four years in office, it was clear to most that his interest in politics was largely confined to himself. In his binary worldview, which contained only winners and losers, many, if not most, of those who voted for him would be described by Trump himself as losers.

Yet in 2020, he received more votes than he did in 2016. He hadn't alienated the country; he'd grown his base, albeit in a losing cause. They were still angry and fearful, and they voted for an angry and fearful man. In our 2019 federal election, Maxime Bernier formed the People's Party of Canada (PPC). This otherwise urbane and stylish politician decided to try a Trump-like approach with the politics of fear. He promised he would fight "extreme multiculturalism," that he would limit "uncontrolled immigration," and fight any motion in Parliament that contained the word "Islamophobia." He was scheduled to attend a rally with the white supremacist Soldiers of Odin (same type of hate group as the Wolves of Odin mentioned earlier, with that Nordic imagery again). The PPC fielded a candidate that called Islam "pure evil."

Mustafa Farooq, executive director of the National Council of Canadian Muslims, noted that Bernier had "engaged in a campaign of misinformation, racism, and dog-whistle politics aimed at Islamophobes."

The PPC failed to win a single seat in the House of Commons, and Bernier even lost his home riding, which he had held for thirteen years. He had initially won that riding with the largest margin of victory for a Conservative Party candidate west of Alberta, with 67% of the votes. His father Gilles had the riding from 1984 to 1997. After his loss, the *Globe and Mail* ran the headline: "Goodbye Maxine Bernier, Canadians have rejected your politics of fear." The message was clear: we are not a country of assholes.

Chapter Eight

Canada's Great Embrace

I N THE AFTERMATH OF 9/11, I FOUND MYSELF in a meeting with Anne McLellan, the Minister of Public Safety and Emergency Preparedness. She and her officials were explaining the rationale for new security measures and approaches in the post-9/11 world, including "preventative arrests," investigative hearings before secret courts, the justification for expanded surveillance powers, and broad no-fly lists. To a lawyer, some of their proposals sounded like they could compromise the rule of law. They would also have a disproportionate impact on Muslim Canadians. There wasn't a focus on identifying and targeting the bad guys.

I was there to provide a perspective on how to protect our country from terrorist threats, but I felt more like the primary target of these new rules. As a lawyer, I heard what sounded like emotional and excessive claims that were being made after 9/11 to justify responses that would actually weaken our democracy rather than strengthen our security. There is no doubt that every credible terrorist threat must be confronted, but we must resist becoming monsters to fight monsters.

The art of leadership in the twenty-first century is to do this without pitting Canadians against one another and threatening our prosperity. So when they told me the government would be able to detain or search people without due process, and that they would assemble a Canadian "no-fly list," I was worried. I asked whether similar risk assessments had been done to quantify the probabilities of other heinous crimes threatening Canadians. There are warnings at swimming pools not to leave kids unattended in change rooms; there are regular missing children alerts. Statistically, these are more credible threats. I pointed out that I had just moved into a new home and my biggest fear was letting my kids out to play in the yard without a fence up to protect them. I wanted to illustrate that there were double standards and a potential bias in how we addressed different public security questions. By their standard, they should help me with my fence to protect my kids from this pressing public safety concern as well. There is nothing more horrific than a terrorist attack, but, to a lawyer, if risk assessments and decisions are going to be made that will have a lasting impact on how we define our society, democracy, and the rule of law for years to come, more rigour should be demanded.

Once we break taboos on freedom and liberty, we are all vulnerable, because society always has a "fringe" and it can define anyone. Just look at what is happening in China with the Uyghurs, the Hong Kongers and now even the Mongolians. Taking out one "fringe" only exposes another in an ultimately self-emulating "nationalist" version of whack-a-mole. History is filled with countless examples where persecution has been used for political gain. Religion, race, clan, skin colour, political belief, sexual preference, and gender have all been used to justify countless horrors. We can all be defined as "the other." The Soviets had a saying: find me the man and I'll find you the crime.

Post-9/11 was an emotional time, and what I sensed in the background to security discussions is that the decision makers were non-Muslim. These policies and practises would never touch their families or loved ones. Perhaps that is why they were so strident and seemed so cavalier about the risks these policies posed.

Time has proven we didn't act wisely. Inaccurate and often useless no-fly lists were created that required tens of millions of dollars to fix. There were shoddy legal tools to detain people in Canada using secret Security Certificates. In the U.S., the FISA (Foreign Intelligence Surveillance Act) warrant process came back to haunt their system. It was designed to target foreigners, but was so broadly worded that almost anyone can be the subject of a FISA warrant for almost any reason. It was what allowed the National Security Agency to collect phone data from Americans for years. In 2015, a FISA warrant was used to investigate Donald Trump's campaign, and the FBI finally admitted to seventeen errors in obtaining a warrant against campaign aide Carter Page. FISA helped widen the glaring divisions in domestic politics and brought into question the fairness of the entire legal system. When these tools were only used against terrorists and innocent foreign nationals, no one cared. But when they are turned on citizens for political gain, or for no particular reason, only then do the issues at stake suddenly became clear. That's what happens when we compromise principles such as the rule of law: it comes back to haunt us all.

Over the years, I've had many meetings with prime ministers and senior ministers on this topic. I worked with an organization of parents, the No Fly List Kids group, which represents thousands of Canadian families whose children and others wrongly remain on Canada's no-fly list. These included a child, Adam Ahmed, who at the age of six was prevented from boarding a flight from Toronto to Boston. He was with his father, Sulemaan, and they were going to watch the Bruins play the Montreal Canadiens. It became a notorious proof of a poorly designed system, one that created largely irrelevant lists that distracted our focus and resources from the real problem and stigmatized a six-year-old hockey fan. I worked with Sulemaan and his wife Khadija Cajee, as well as my eminent litigation partner, Sheila Block, to make the case to the prime minister's office that it was time to fix the system, ending this mistreatment of our own citizens and strengthening our national security by focusing on the real problem.

*

The rule of law is the key organizing principle of our society. This was reaffirmed in our meetings with government officials when Sheila reminded them that we could either all find a logical way to fix these no-fly lists or she could take the matter to the court up the street to ask their opinion. In Ottawa, that court up the street is the Supreme Court, and we were confident we would agree that there must be a better way to craft no-fly lists, one that protects Canadians without abusing them. Our courts provide the checks and balances that protect us from political excesses. Democracies come in many shapes and sizes, but, at their core, they all have a place, an independent court of law, where the peasant can contest the king and the peasant can still prevail. Where you have that, you have the rule of law and rule of institutions rather than the rule of a man and his whims or the risk of mob rule.

Our efforts were successful. Now we have a "Canadian Traveller Number" application system that simply allows Canadians to con-firm their identity and eliminate false positive no-fly list matches. We can focus on the real threats and let innocent Canadians like Adam go to a hockey game with his dad. It is a shame it required more than $81 million of Canadian taxpayer money to fix a prob-lem that could have been prevented in the first place. The original Public Safety Act that established these lists was enacted by a Liberal government and expanded under Conservative govern-ments, so both parties share the blame.

I had met Stephen Harper at a few public events, but also on two private occasions. The first was in 2004 when he was oppos-ition leader. I was excited about the chance to speak to him directly about the Conservative Party under his leadership, and the place of Muslims in Canada. Being from Alberta, I grew up in a conserv-ative province under Conservative governments, although I don't see the world in strict ideological terms. I'm open to good people from almost anywhere on the political spectrum who want to serve our country.

But in the post-9/11 world, I had seen the federal Conservative Party and conservative politics in general develop an amorphous cloud of mistrust towards *all* Muslims and Islam. This was par-ticularly hurtful because of my Albertan identity. I saw the world in much the same way as other Albertans. I never imagined that I was an "other" Canadian or a stranger. It was like looking into a mirror that is somehow lying to you. So I was looking forward to a face-to-face conversation with Harper.

Much to my disappointment, the meeting was uneventful. Harper didn't engage and came across as detached and unemotional.

I tried to find some common ground in our mutual connection to Alberta. I remarked that even though he was from Calgary and I was from Edmonton, it was okay for us to put our city rivalries aside in Ottawa. That didn't work. I tried to find common political ground, describing many in the Muslim community as conservative and entrepreneurial and open to the Conservative party. I jokingly asked whether the Conservative party had an allergy to potential votes. There were, after all, a million Muslims in the country. My attempts at humour landed like an anvil on a concrete floor. The meeting fizzled and came to a merciful end. It was interesting that the assembled group still wanted a photo to commemorate the event. I obliged the picture, although it wasn't something I wanted to memorialize. I assumed it was used for some political purpose. The lesson I took away from that meeting was to be careful about becoming a prop in someone else's play.

My next meeting was in 2006. Harper was Prime Minister now and had convened a meeting of Muslim Canadian "leaders" in the wake of the Toronto 18 terror investigation. Again, Mr. Harper seemed detached. I poured my heart out, pointing out that Muslims had a long history in Canada, and as proud Canadians had as much interest in the security of our country as anyone else. Criminals from all backgrounds commit crimes every year; why did Muslim criminals have to define all Muslim Canadians? It was soon clear that the meeting wasn't going to lead anywhere. This time I didn't stick around for the picture.

That the glaring publicity accompanying a small group of unsuccessful Muslim terrorists threatened to mar a century of mutual respect illustrated how fragile the Canadian mosaic can be. It became even more fragile after the introduction of anti-terrorism legislation. In 2015, Prime Minister Harper's Bill C-51 was passed in the House of Commons. It had been prompted, in part, by two incidents in 2014. On October 20, Martin Couture-Rouleau rammed his car into two Canadian soldiers in Saint-Jean-sur-Richelieu, Quebec. He had been radicalized after converting to Islam, and an ISIS spokesman had asked for vehicular homicide to be perpetrated. It was viewed as an act of terrorism.

Two days later there was a shooting on Parliament Hill and inside the Parliament buildings that left one soldier and the shooter dead. Harper labelled it a terrorist act. Bill C-51 was passed four months later, with the Liberals on board. It gave CSIS a mandate to "disrupt terror plots" and expand no-fly list powers. It would give the government greater powers to stop "violent Islamic jihadi terrorists." Public Safety Minister Steven Blaney said the expanded powers would only be used if there were reasonable grounds to believe an activity was a threat to the nation's security.

This turned out not to be true, unfortunately. Thousands of people with no links to terrorism found themselves on no-fly lists, including children and an Emergency Room physician who tried to take his family to Disneyland. Lawyer Faisal Kutty complained that Canadian Muslims could be found "too guilty to fly, but too innocent to charge." Those who were prevented from flying weren't allowed to see the evidence against them.

Bill C-51 was a political bill, designed and introduced to allay public fears. But it did little to increase public safety and damaged legal and democratic ideals. At its worst, it marginalized people who were vulnerable, potentially exacerbating the threat of radicalization.

In Quebec, Bill 21 was tabled, known as the province's secularism bill, which bans religious symbols in parts of the civil service. This was seen by the Muslim community to be targeted at them, specifically women wearing the hijab. After the bill was tabled, there was a spike in harassment against Muslims, and fears that the bill would heighten or support Islamophobia. Immigration Minister Simon Jolin-Barrette, who sponsored the bill, said, "The secularism bill encourages better living together." But it appeared to have the opposite effect. When the government marginalizes its own citizens, "better living together" isn't a likely outcome. Terrorism is a serious problem, but legislation that targets thousands of innocent citizens isn't the way to combat it. A cynical observer might say the government is aware of this and is looking for votes among a resentful white population. Certainly we have seen this in the United States.

Whatever my past encounters with Mr. Harper, and despite my feelings for the legislation he put through, I have great respect for the office of Prime Minister. And I would have another unexpected meeting with him.

*

The Commissioner of the Canadian Football League, Mark Cohon, had attended Toronto's Upper Canada College; in 2012, he reached out to his alma mater and offered an Upper Canada College football MVP the chance to be anointed CFL Commissioner-for-a-Day. My son Mohamad was quarterbacking one of the UCC teams at the time, and, as it turned out, was named the MVP of a tournament.

Mohamad was thrilled that he was going to be the CFL Commissioner-for-a-Day, and I was as thrilled as he was. I'd grown up watching the Edmonton Eskimos during their glory years in the 1970s. I was part of the Knothole Gang, kids who got cheap seats in the endzone bleachers at the old Clarke Stadium in Edmonton. It was an intimate setting, and it felt like we were in the middle of the game, almost playing. It was always cold near the end of the season, snow wasn't out of the question, but the excitement of the game was enough to keep us warm. I can still remember our quarterback, Tom Wilkinson, the least athletic-looking player in the league, dissecting opposing defences with surgical precision.

As Commissioner-for-a-Day, Mohamad shadowed Mark, going to meetings, going out for lunch. Mohamad loved it, and he asked Mark when his term was going to be up. That evening, Mark invited our family to his box to watch the last game of the regular season. It was an exciting game. Chad Owens, quarterback for the hometown Argos, set the record for most all-purpose yards in a regular season. Mark and my son talked football, and at the end of the game, Mark asked whether Mohamad would like to participate in the upcoming 100th Anniversary Grey Cup Game. Of course, he said.

We didn't get many details about what the ceremonies would entail, but in the days leading up to the game, some consent forms showed up in my inbox. It was a busy week in my law practice, so I quickly scanned and signed the attachment, and didn't pay much attention to the details. I was reminded of the old adage "the shoemaker's children go without shoes." While I spend most days crossing every "t" and dotting every "i" for my clients, I often don't have time to do that for myself, which is why I also live by the adage: "only a fool lawyer would have himself as a client."

It was such an overwhelming honour to have Mohamad involved that I didn't really care what role he was going to play. The more meaningful point was what this represented to me and our country. In the post-9/11 world, some Canadians were now telling Muslim Canadians "to go back home." This new sectarianism reminded me of the kind I'd seen in other countries. It isn't necessarily born from hate, but from a misguided and shallow form of cultural pride that seduces people to exclude and marginalize others. It was symbolic that Mark Cohon, a leading Jewish Canadian, was asking Mohamad Assaf, a young Muslim Canadian, to be part of such an historic Canadian event.

Sunday, November 25 finally arrived, and we were told to go to the Royal York Hotel early in the morning to meet the game ceremony production team and get instructions on the day's plan. Mohamad and I arrived, and they gave us the event timetable and showed us where to access the stadium and how to get to field level. We were told to meet as a group again at 2 p.m. for an on-field rehearsal.

The next event on the schedule was the Commissioner's Brunch, to which Mohamad and I were kindly invited. It looked like it was going to be a nice event, but it's not often I have my twelve-year-old son to myself without a hockey rink or soccer field to rush to, so I was thinking we would quietly skip the brunch and grab a burger and some chicken wings and spend some private time together. Given the size of the event, I figured we wouldn't be missed.

Just as we were about to skip quietly away, one of the organizers tapped me on the shoulder and told me to make sure Mohamad and I sat at a table close to the presentation stage.

"Why?" I asked.

"So that Mohamad can get up onto the stage easily."

I mentally rifled through all the emails I'd read and couldn't recall anything about Mohamad being up on stage. She read the perplexed look on my face.

"You know," she said, "to formally be presented with the Canadian flag from the Governor General on behalf of all Canadian youth."

It only then dawned on me that Mohamad's role was bigger than I'd imagined. The Canadian flag on behalf of all Canadian youth? The Governor General? It came into focus. Mohamad was going to be a representative of ALL Canadian youth and carry the Canadian flag to midfield as part of the opening ceremonies.

The beauty and meaning of what was about to unfold started to register. I was floored. Country, history, sport, and family, all these connections of identity and belonging brought together in this unexpected experience. I found a couple of seats near the stage and, as we sat down, I noticed Prime Minister Stephen Harper sitting nearby. I asked Mohamad if he wanted to meet the PM. He would have been much more excited to meet Wayne Gretzky, but managed to say the right thing.

The Prime Minister was just finishing one of his courses, so it was a good time to interrupt him briefly. I lightly tapped him on the shoulder and he kindly stood up to say hello. I said it was nice to see him again. He didn't appear to remember me, but I wasn't the person who mattered today. I introduced him to Mohamad, and said he was going to have the honour of carrying out the Canadian flag to midfield in the opening ceremonies, representing all Canadian youth.

The PM's demeanour immediately changed. He quickly warmed and was very gracious to Mohamad. It was a special Canadian moment, and Harper himself insisted we take a picture together. He called over his official photographer. This time, I was happy to pose and afterwards I told him that it would be extra special if he could send us a signed copy. He promised he would. A part of me also wanted him to reflect, as he wrote the name Mohamad, how Canadian a Mohamad could be.

A few weeks later, a signed picture with a personalized message to Mohamad and me arrived. It remains in my office as a warm reminder of that day.

The brunch continued, and Mohamad was called up on the stage. The ceremony to present the flag to him was conducted by the Governor General, David Johnston, a naturally warm man. After the ceremony, he found Mohamad and joked that he may need some help with the ceremonial kick-off because he wasn't the athlete he once was (he had played hockey for Harvard) and may need some youthful help.

It was time to go to the stadium for the on-field rehearsal. We started to feel the weight of the event, the enormity of the spectacle of the 100th Anniversary of the Grey Cup. The Queen had issued a message, diplomatically wishing good luck to both teams. Burton Cummings was scheduled to sing the national anthem. The half-time entertainment featured Justin Bieber, Carly Rae Jepsen, and Canadian legend Gordon Lightfoot. It would be the most watched Grey Cup in history—almost half the country tuned in for some portion of the game. Hundreds of people were involved in producing and organizing the event. It was hard to imagine how this 12-year-old boy, and the slice of Canadian history he represented, was going to be worked into such a massive production. Almost eighty-five years after my great-grandfather came to Canada to make a life for himself and future generations, I was about to watch his great-great-grandson have the honour of carrying the Canadian flag on behalf of Canadian youth. I thought of my great-grandfather and the immense embrace Canada had shown him and was now showing my son. And I wondered if we would always be embraced this way.

Chapter Nine

Taking the Canadian Spirit Abroad

MY INTEREST IN LAW WAS FORMED at a young age. At the age of nine, I built up the courage to tell my father I no longer wanted to be an architect. He was in the real estate development business at the time and wanted an architect in the family. It felt like a really big thing in my nine-year-old mind, although probably not as big a deal to him. Years later, I was excited to be going to law school. I wanted to learn how societies organized themselves, because laws are the building blocks of any civilization. But the laws are more than a stack of books or words on a page. They require the necessary institutions and political culture to animate those words in a way that is true to their meaning. If these qualities are in place, the law can serve as the instrument of civil and economic progress.

Twenty-five years of practicing competition law has given me a particular insight into how we balance personal versus collective goals and values. Competition law is mostly about ensuring that no firm has a monopoly and that markets remain competitive in order for consumers to get the best products at the best prices. But in Canada there is an exception to this golden rule. This exception, unsurprisingly, is rooted in examining whether we are collectively better off. The Efficiencies Defence is meant to calculate whether a merger of two businesses would benefit more

Canadians than it would harm, even if it gives one firm a monopoly or a formidable competitive position. If it is determined that more Canadians would likely benefit from the broader economic efficiencies of a merger, even an anti-competitive one, we have rules to allow it. These cases are rare and hard to prove, but I've been involved in the two leading ones, including one of which went all the way up to the Supreme Court.

In the second year of my law practice, I was summoned to get involved in a propane merger known as the *Superior Propane Case*. Propane isn't the sexiest of industries, but this case was fought for years over the application of the Efficiencies Defence. It was found that although the merger could, potentially, harm certain propane customers, but that it would also create spin-off efficiency benefits. Those efficiencies meant the newly merged company would use fewer trucks, equipment, and other resources. These savings could potentially lead to lower prices for those "saved resources" because they would free up those trucks and resources for other Canadians to then be able to use in their businesses. The court saw that the merger would do more good than harm in the broader economy, and it was approved. This sense of the collective is uniquely Canadian. South Africa is one of the few other countries in the world that has this Efficiencies Defence, and it was borrowed from Canada.

The Efficiencies Defence is a product of our unique culture and principles, which is maybe why it was attractive to post-apartheid South Africa. It reflects the society and economy they were trying to create. In seeking the fairest outcomes possible, it is always prudent to pause and ask, through a formal and measured process, if it attains the best outcome for all citizens. The answer is secondary to the fact that we ask.

South Africa wasn't the only country interested in our particularly Canadian perspective on competition law. Early in my career, I was summoned to a meeting with senior partners at my firm regarding an assignment they were trying to secure from the World Bank. The World Bank was considering us to advise the Kingdom of Jordan on how to draft a competition law. It was part of a package of reforms necessary for Jordan to join a trade pact with the European Union. The World Bank asked whether our firm had any Arabic-speaking competition lawyers. At the time, I was the only fluent Arabic-speaking competition lawyer in Canada, maybe one of the few in the Western world. It was certainly a short list, but Canada had produced one, and we got the mandate.

I spent the next three years going to Jordan on a regular basis with senior partners to draft a competition law. It was one of the greatest experiences of my life. It was also nice that I was able to visit an aunt who lived there. Even at that early point in my career, I saw that Canadians were professionally respected, and that people put trust in our perspective. I also recognized how valuable this reputation was. Throughout my career, the Canadian brand has been like a wind in my sail as I worked around the world. It would become even more crucial to my later work in Dubai, helping to open the first offices for any Canadian law firm there.

I made my first visit to Dubai in 2002. It had embarked on an aggressive advertising campaign to bring people to the city. The iconic image of its sail-shaped hotel, the Burj Al Arab on Dubai's coast, was everywhere at the time. Dubai was running out of oil and eager to transition from a resource-based economy. It wanted to become a global business hub. When I arrived in the city, I saw posters claiming that Dubai would be a crossroads to the world. It was hard to believe that this small Middle Eastern outpost would be the crossroads to anything. Yet, somehow, in less than twenty years, it did become a global logistics and tourism hub, and one of the main connectors between West and East.

I had learned to speak Arabic at home and it served me well on trips to Lebanon in the summer to see my grandparents, each of whom had a profound impact on me; they taught me the value of a strong work ethic, respect, grit, compassion, and love. I never imagined speaking Arabic would be of any professional value. Back then, the economic power of the global economy was all in the West, and it didn't look like things would change in my lifetime. No one could have guessed that within thirty years, the world would see the greatest transfer of wealth from West to East in human history. In 2020, the Asian economies became larger than the rest of the world combined. We have seen the emergence of important city hubs like Shanghai, Mumbai, and Dubai. In the wake of the financial crisis, I often heard the rhyming names of those cities whenever an unemployed banker wondered about where they should look for their next job.

For business lawyers, too, it is important to always keep your eye on where business and the markets are going, not just where they are today. Wayne Gretzky's hockey advice to "watch where the puck is going rather than where it's at" applies here too. Dubai was in a strong international position, and competition was tough. Businesspeople and law firms from around the world were clamouring to enter the market.

While the United Arab Emirates (UAE), home to the glittering city of Dubai, is in some respects another world, it does share some similarities with Canada, especially regarding its relative level of tolerance to other some other countries in the Middle East. On the beach, you see burkas next to bikinis. You can go to a mosque or a nightclub or both. How did this little-known, young (48-year-old) country attract so many diverse people to invest their futures here? Of their ten million people, almost nine million are immigrants. It's often explained as an instance of "build it and they will come," but the globe is littered with white elephant projects. Building is easy. Attracting and keeping people is hard. Russia spent almost $50 billion to build Sochi for the Winter Olympics in the hopes it would become a top tourist destination. It didn't. To keep people coming, there is a human factor involved that no amount of PR hype can replicate. It's just a feeling you get, a feeling similar to what my great-grandfather had when he came to Canada decades ago: that you are welcome and anything is possible.

I began to spend time in the region seeking work for my Canadian law firm, Ogilvy Renault. I received one of my major projects from a Canadian working in a UAE government department; he was sick of seeing that only big U.S. and European law firms were advising them. He initially called me in hopes of getting a Canadian firm considered. We ended up winning the mandate to help develop the laws in the telecom industry.

Then in 2008 and in the midst of the global financial crisis, another law firm approached me with a new opportunity to open an office in the United Arab Emirates. It was a rare opportunity to use both my legal and business skills to open the first Canadian law office there. I began by filling out countless forms with multiple regulators, slowly assembling all the pieces to obtain a law practice license. Over the course of a few months, it became apparent that waiting patiently in line wasn't going to be enough. There was a final, crucial step to the approval process that was a matter of pure discretion by the director of the Ruler's Court. No amount of properly completed forms could compel him to approve us.

The main issue was the intense competition for these scarce licenses. My request was being drowned out by the requests of competing global law firms. I needed to get to the director so that I could make my case. But how to get to him? I was told it was impossible to get a meeting unless he asked to meet you. I would have to work my way up the chain of command and one day, hopefully, get summoned.

It looked like my turn was never going to come. To complicate matters, the UAE was in a full-out diplomatic war with Canada because of a falling out over the airline landing rights of Emirates Airlines in Canada. Dubai felt it was being restricted for the benefit of Air Canada. The dispute escalated to the point where the UAE, after years of defence collaboration, banned Canada from using its Camp Mirage, the military logistics base that Canada had set up in 2001. It also forbade Defence Minister Peter MacKay from flying over the UAE on a trip back from Afghanistan.

The last day before I had to return to Toronto, I finished a meeting with another government department with no progress. I drew upon my Lebanese heritage, which taught me that hearing the word "no" only prompts the question "Who said so?" I left the meeting and jumped into a taxi to the Ruler's Court so that I could cold call the director. Arriving in a taxi was already a knock against me. If I'd been more important, I would have arrived in a limousine.

It was a typical steaming hot day and traffic was jammed and it didn't help that the taxi's air-conditioning was barely working. I didn't look as pressed as I would have wanted. The Ruler's Court had armed guards at the gate. I tried to keep things low key and disappear into the back seat, hoping the taxi driver's explanation that he was merely dropping off his passenger would get us through.

It quickly became clear that this wasn't going to work. The guard gestured for the driver to lower the rear window so he could see and speak to me. The driver lowered the window and the barrel of the guard's machine gun stared back at me.

Staring into the machine gun, I adjusted my request. Instead of asking to meet with the director, I said I wanted to meet with one of his assistants. I had in fact spoken to her, although she'd told me that it would not be possible to meet with her boss. For some reason, the guard let me pass.

It was an older building and had no directory to guide me to the floor of the director's office. It wasn't the kind of place where people showed up without an appointment. Having made it this far, I didn't want to draw more attention to myself and get turned back, so I walked past the small reception desk at the entrance as though I knew where I was going. The people at the desk looked like they were busy with something else, anyway. I next went looking for a janitor or someone to help me figure out the floor that the director's office was on. On my third try, I found someone who could help me and jumped into the elevator.

When the elevator doors opened, it was like walking into a different world. These offices were vast and were much more organized and modern. There was an immediate reception area and what looked like layers of other reception areas beyond. I approached the first desk and asked to meet the director. I said that I'd come a very long way from Canada and it was my last day before I had to return to report to my partners on the project. I told her my only priority was to meet the director to discuss obtaining a potential license. My request instilled a combined sense of surprise, fear, and confusion in the face of the receptionist. It appeared she had never entertained a cold call like this. She may have been wondering how I had gotten through the first gate. She went to consult with others and, after what seemed like an eternity of standing alone in awkward silence, waiting for a verdict, she came back to tell me the director would almost certainly not be able to see me but I was free to wait in an adjacent boardroom.

She led me to a small boardroom. They didn't offer me coffee or water, which was out of character for Dubai hospitality. Typically, at the start of every meeting, you're offered a long list coffees, teas, and beverages. It was clear they were hoping I wasn't going to stay long. I opened my briefcase and pulled out documents to read while I waited.

Hours passed. I arrived at the offices at 11 a.m. and every hour the receptionist would come in and repeat that the director was very busy and it didn't look like he would be able to meet me. I politely replied that I had nothing else to do and there was nothing more important than meeting him and I was happy to wait. Every hour we repeated this ritual.

While I was waiting, I didn't dare get up to go to the restroom or ask for anything, worried that once I left the room I'd be escorted out. So there I sat, hour after hour. At 4 p.m. she came back again to say it was only thirty minutes before closing and the director was still not available to meet and strongly encouraged me to leave. Again, I told her I was happy to wait until they closed for any chance to meet with him.

Fifteen minutes later, the receptionist returned. I thought she was going to turn off the lights and tell me to scram. To my great surprise, she said the director would be able to see me for ten minutes for a brief conversation. I couldn't believe it. Suddenly I felt like the dog that caught the car: how was I going to convince him to give me a license in ten minutes? What could I tell him to break through the noise of all the other sales pitches he'd heard?

I was escorted into a big boardroom and told to sit and wait. Again no one offered me water or coffee, emphasizing that this would be quick. When the director entered and took a seat at the head of the long boardroom table, he was courteous but clearly detached. He avoided making eye contact to prevent me from becoming too comfortable. I looked at him while he looked down at the notepad he'd brought, ostensibly to make notes. I cleared my throat and told him my firm had almost a century of success in Canada but hadn't yet opened an office outside the country. When we finally decided to make that historic first international step, we chose Dubai because of the opportunity and the global business hub it had become. I tied my story to those ads I'd seen in the Dubai airport when I first visited, and the pride they must have felt in realizing that original vision. I told him as a Canadian of Arab descent, how personally important it was to me to help build another important commercial bridge between Dubai and Canada. While Dubai may not have needed another Western law firm, it was missing that connection to Canadian business leaders.

Dubai is a lot like Canada, I continued, a place where immigrants come seeking better opportunities. I told him that my great-grandfather came to Canada in the early part of the last century and it had embraced him and given him an opportunity to build a future that was not possible for him in Lebanon. Dubai now provided that same opportunity, attracting millions from around the globe who left their homes to forge a new future in Dubai.

After I stopped speaking, there was a pause before he spoke in a soft and reassuring tone, telling me to write him a letter that reflected the words I had just said, after which "what I would like to see would happen." And that's how I got the license to allow the first Canadian law firm to open a practice in Dubai. After that, I went on to get the first licenses for a Canadian law firm in Abu Dhabi and Doha, Qatar. In this century, difference has become power.

My experiences opening offices in the Gulf and being engaged to advise on global matters have confirmed to me the value of our Canadian brand. This goodwill was hard-earned and needs to be strategically nurtured. It's not simple for a middle power like Canada to punch above its weight on the global stage. The value Canada brings to the world goes back decades. In the aftermath of World War II, the world was largely divided by the two great remaining powers, the United States and the Soviet Union. At the Yalta talks, Stalin was so aggressive in dividing the spoils and extending the Soviet sphere of influence that Roosevelt reminded him that "even the eagle lets the sparrow sing." His message was clear: influence, yes, complete occupation and control of others, no.

One sparrow that continued to sing was Canada. We saw it in the country's role in the 1956 Suez Canal Crisis. Egyptian leader Gamal Abdel Nasser was accepting arms from the Soviets and denouncing the West. As a result, the foreign investment he needed to build the Aswan Dam on the Nile River vanished. Nasser then seized control of the Suez Canal, a vital shipping route that was run by foreign interests, mostly French and British, and boldly announced that Egypt would no longer be under "the domination of the imperialists."

In October of that year, Israel invaded Egypt. Days later, British and French bombers leveled Egyptian airfields. Khrushchev threatened to use nuclear weapons if the French and British didn't withdraw. War was imminent.

The United Nations met to discuss the situation, and it was a Canadian, Lester Pearson, the Minister of External Affairs, who came up with A plan whereby the French and British both withdrew, but an international peacekeeping force would remain in the area. Despite objections from the British, all fifty-seven member nations voted in favour. The force was also commanded by a Canadian, General E. L. M. Burns. It was an international triumph. Pearson won a Nobel Peace Prize in 1957 for his leadership and vision, which he accepted on behalf of all Canadians.

Today the world is more complex and multipolar. We must take into account rising powers such as China, the revanchism of Russia, and the sheer size of India. Unfortunately, as our complexity increases, leadership is retreating. Canada can continue to be that sparrow, setting the tune for the next generation of peace and prosperity. Our time has truly come.

PART IV
CHANGING THE STORY

Chapter Ten
Social Media's Dangerous New World

YOU KNOW THINGS HAVE GOTTEN A BIT SQUIRRELLY when a religion is blamed for climate change. That was the message in 2016 when the *Conservative Fans* website started the rumor that the Islamic State was responsible for Fort McMurray's devastating wildfires. Fort McMurray is home to Canada's oil sands, but it is also home to one of the largest mosques in the country, and a thriving Muslim community that includes some of my own relatives. The internet has given license to a lot of things, and hatred is, unfortunately, among them.

How do you feel when someone constantly tells a lie about you and can broadcast that lie on global platforms like Facebook or Google? Do you get angry? Do you feel sad? Do you just give up?

In Canada, we are often smug about the fact that we don't have the kind of toxic racism that plagues our southern neighbours. But a report issued by the Institute for Strategic Dialogue in the U.K. identified more than 6,600 online pages, accounts, or groups in Canada that were spreading white supremacist or misogynistic views. On a per capita basis, Canada was shown to be one of the most active countries in the world when it came to spreading toxic views. Among the sites flagged by the U.K. group were the "Three Percenters," an Islamophobic armed militia group. Another anti-Muslim movement is the Canadian Defence

League, which describes itself as "fighting back against high Muslim immigration levels."

One of the blogs read: "How stupid are we? We allow our government to flood our nation with Muslims, give them welfare for life (with multiple wives), and then tell us that we must not offend them 'or we will go to prison.' Islamic immigration has destroyed every country in Europe, and it will destroy both Canada and the U.S. Are we so stupid that we'll stand by and watch this happen in our country?"

In many ways, the world seems to be dividing again. While the Berlin Wall fell more than thirty years ago, a new Cold War is brewing. Once more it is challenging belief and trust in free, open, and liberal societies. Russian President Vladimir Putin stated that the idea of Western liberalism had "become obsolete." The old Cold War was waged with military build-ups and proxy wars on foreign shores. The new Cold War is being waged on the invisible, complicated battlefields of cyberspace. Karl Marx once noted that "we will hang the capitalists with the rope they sell us." The rope we sold them was the unrivalled freedom of the Internet. And now we are clicking, searching, liking, and friending ourselves to death.

In some ways, Facebook and Google have become modern Trojan Horses of our own making. How can sharing birthday photos with my grandmother or searching for a new pair of shoes threaten my way of life? Because it can also represent a propaganda network deployed to divide and conquer our open and diverse societies.

The only thing the old Communists were better at than us was the art of propaganda, and their successors in Russia still have the skills. American intelligence agencies determined conclusively that Russians interfered in the 2016 election. They hacked Hillary Clinton's campaign, staged rallies in places like Florida and Pennsylvania, spread propaganda on YouTube, Instagram, and Facebook, and paid for ads criticizing Clinton. The Senate Intelligence Committee's report noted that the Russians "were in a position to, at a minimum, alter or delete voter registration data." The aim was to boost Trump's chances of victory and to sow distrust in the very idea of democracy. The ground was fertile for these seeds of distrust, and the technology made it relatively easy to accomplish.

I watched the 2016 Democratic nomination debates through the lens of a competition lawyer. The fact that there were only three people on that stage seemed odd to me. How could it be that an open competition for the leader of a political party, someone who essentially has a fifty percent chance of becoming the most powerful person in the world, could only attract three candidates? Only one of them was a high-profile candidate, Hillary Clinton, with two relative unknowns in Bernie Sanders and Martin O'Malley. The Republican Party had seventeen candidates; the field was so large that the party had to split it into separate debates to manage the process.

It seemed clear that one process had a greater risk of producing an even more market-distorted outcome. One process was dictating to its market what they would get, while the other attempted to reflect what the market wanted. It turned out the market was most sick of what it perceived as inauthentic and scripted politicians and members of political dynasties. I believe what political experts underestimated in the 2016 election (but what the market told them) was the single overriding demand of the people was for some kind of authenticity. The biggest surprise here was that people were so desperate to vote for authenticity that they were willing to go with an authentic liar. The power of Donald Trump's candidacy wasn't in his leadership or his ability to create something. It was his ability to tap into something and nurture it and that is what made it so difficult to take him down. He was a symbol and this why many of his supporters saw attacks on him as attacks on them. He was their political battering ram against an out-of-touch establishment system.

In contrasting competition terms, it appeared that the forces of "Democratic party market dominance" were working to exclude other competing candidates from effectively participating. Even with all that, Bernie Sanders came close to beating Hillary Clinton; in many ways he embodied the same outsider qualities and authenticity that Trump rode on the Republican side. But Sanders couldn't break through the Democratic Party power apparatus and the Clinton coronation mindset. With any product or service market, you can prevent the better mousetrap getting to market, but it's the consumers (or voters in this case) who ultimately pay a higher price for a lower quality product. This is essentially why government authorities are going after market dominant technology platforms like Google and Facebook. The issues raised aren't much different in the "market" of democratic elections.

In a game where the winning candidates from each party are then thrown into the biggest market test—an election—one can see how a candidate from a smaller field, one that has been more insulated from broader outside market forces, risks having the more difficult time. If the objective of the game is to win in an open vote (in a non-incumbent year) it would seem better for that party to hold a genuinely open leadership campaign and start market testing their candidates as early as possible. This way they can ensure the candidate and the party are less likely to be out of touch with the current needs of the people. They need to benefit from the healthy market feedback loop that a genuinely open nomination process brings. So, detached from the names or personalities of any candidate, a competition lawyer might have guessed that whichever candidate came out of the more open and democratic nomination process would be more likely to win in the bigger election game. That is what happened with President Trump's 2016 election victory.

It was then ironic, at least from a market point of view, to see part of Trump's 2020 election loss resulted from him making it harder for his voters (his customers) to buy his product (vote for him). He told them not to vote using the easy mail-in option, and essentially told his customers, in the midst of a pandemic, that you can only buy my product in-store and not online. He ignored a basic lesson of retail: never make it harder for customers to buy your product. He handily lost the popular vote, but only lost the Electoral College by a few hundred thousand votes across a handful of states. If he had told his supporters to vote by mail, perhaps a few hundred thousand of them in the right states could have put him over the top in the Electoral College. He also lost because this time the Democratic Party had a wide-open nomination and produced a candidate who had authenticity as well as the ability to bring calm to the chaos.

In 2016, market distortion was already in play before the Russians even began to use our readily available social platforms to distort democracy. At that point, it was just a matter of tactics. Two key ingredients to effective propaganda are knowing your audience and being able to reach them in large numbers. Modern digital platforms are essentially big vaults of data that know more about us than we know ourselves, and they reach almost every one of us daily. And like moths to a flame, we can't resist.

The Russians favoured Trump because of his utility as a useful idiot. And perhaps there was some leverage to compromise him. Trump, who is quick to criticize both friends and foe, has never said a bad word about Putin. You don't need to deploy Google's infamous algorithms to see a pattern.

The term useful idiot first originated in Russia, often attributed to Lenin, and refers to someone who may be useful to a cause without actually comprehending their own role. Trump, with his narcissism and adolescent insecurities, was a perfect candidate. But now we are all in danger of becoming useful idiots.

When it comes to the dissemination of information, we have largely trusted the owners and managers of dominant digital platforms. While trust is good, Reagan shrewdly said at the end of the last Cold War, "trust, but verify." Now it's time to verify. We need to take thoughtful steps to regulate the excesses and potential harm to our politics and economy from these twenty-first century platforms. We need to bring a balance between the benefits and risks of this new technology and its dominance and influence.

*

In August 2020, the CEOs of Facebook, Amazon, Apple, and Google endured a six-hour grilling from Congress about data and competition concerns. David Cicilline, Chairman of the House Antitrust Committee, ended the Congressional Antitrust Hearing by quoting U.S. Supreme Court Justice Louis Brandeis, who said, "We can have democracy in this country, or we can have great wealth concentrated in the hands of a few, but we can't have both." At the time of the hearing, Jeff Bezos, the CEO of Amazon, had a net worth of $188 billion, more than the combined budgets of 18 U.S. states. The top five American tech firms had a market cap of US $7.6 trillion. Brandeis, who died in 1941, would have rolled over in his grave.

Watching the hearing, the market equivalent of escape velocity came to mind. What happens if a platform gains enough momentum to escape the gravitational pull of market forces and can operate untethered from meaningful competition and democratic tolerances? Like a giant among mere mortals, the natural movements of the big tech companies, Google, Facebook, Apple, and Microsoft, can accidently (or purposely) destroy what's around them.

The health of any economy is rooted in how productive it is. Productivity is not a cold economic term but a concept that captures all the meaningful things that people do in a society when they have the fewest barriers in their way. These barriers include race, religion, poor education, or health. They also include market entry barriers because big companies won't always let you in or they can unfairly put you out of business. When I teach competition law, I always remind students not to mistake every business outcome as a genuine market event. The *Titanic* was a worthy vessel and could have sailed for decades if its captain had just veered a bit to the right.

Governments maintain and promote free markets so we can all figure out what we are best at and cater to the needs and wants of fellow citizens. They foster an environment where innovation thrives and we have access to the necessary tools and technology to do what we want and need to do, like using computers rather than the abacus. We need everyone to be connected in the twenty-first century economy in the same way that the railroads and highways connected the economies of the past.

Competition market analysis shows innovation and competitive entry are not easy, especially when key gatekeepers are also competitors. Big tech is at a critical juncture. If the big firms don't self-correct and regulate themselves, then competition regulators will take action. It's just a matter of how drastic the moves will be. There is already blood is in the water. To level the playing field, the European Commission is proposing regulations that would designate dominant tech platforms as "gatekeepers" that would require them to, among other things, ensure their systems are interoperable and open to others under the threat of penalties, including divestiture.

The grilling from Congress was primarily theatre, a chance for politicians to appear as if they were doing something to help the average consumer. But the heavy lifting will be done by lawyers rather than politicians. It appeared there had been some real market investigation done prior to the hearing (Amazon's acquisition of its competitor Diaper.com, and Facebook's of its competitor Instagram, are prime examples). The issues for each company are quite different, but it's clear that new rules and antitrust enforcement approaches will have to be drawn up to accommodate the internet era. The historic court cases launched against Facebook and Google will also expose much of what is at stake.

"These companies as they exist today have monopoly power," said David Cicilline. "Some need to be broken up, all need to be properly regulated and held accountable. We need to ensure the antitrust laws, first written more than a century ago, work in the digital age."

*

It's worth going back a century to look at the case that those original laws were written for. One hundred and ten years ago, the U.S. Supreme Court made one of its most famous decisions in competition and antitrust law. That decision coined the term "trustbusting" and gave birth to what we consider modern competition law. On May 15, 1911, the U.S. Supreme Court ordered the break-up of John D. Rockefeller's Standard Oil Trust. It controlled forty-one companies and was responsible for the refining of more than 90 percent of all oil in the United States. The court found that Standard Oil's size and tactics represented an "unreasonable restraint" of trade on the market.

When Standard Oil was formed in 1870, oil was mainly used to make kerosene for lamps. There were dozens of oil companies, most of them centred in Pennsylvania. Competition was stiff, and not all those companies were profitable. Rockefeller understood this and moved quickly to take control of the industry. On New Year's Day, 1872, Rockefeller was able to borrow enough capital from the banks to force most of his competitors to either sell to him or be ruined by him.

He adopted the tactics of Genghis Khan, who first tried to intimidate his enemies into surrendering. If they did, they were treated well. If they resisted, they were destroyed. He met with his competitors and pointed out that the oil refining business was overpopulated and most companies would go bankrupt, anyway. He had the money to buy them out at a fair price, and he also had the clout to manipulate shipping rates and get a better deal for Standard Oil. In three months, Rockefeller bought out twenty-two of his twenty-six Cleveland competitors. It became known as "the Cleveland Massacre." By 1900, it wasn't clear what could stop the growth of Standard Oil. Rockefeller had retired but Standard Oil looked set to continue its growth trajectory forever. By this time, it had withstood various antitrust cases and paid some hefty fines for its conduct, yet still managed to remain intact.

It was only through the efforts of a "muckraking" journalist, Ida Tarbell, who wrote a series of articles for *McClure's* (published in book form as *The History of the Standard Oil Company*) that public outrage was mobilized and the company's momentum was checked. Her groundbreaking work set the stage for the Supreme Court to order the break-up of Standard Oil. The case gave birth to competition laws and policy that shaped business in the twentieth century. Why was Ida so interested? As a child, she had seen the "Cleveland Massacre" firsthand. One of those victims was her father. Talk about an unintended consequence.

One of the parallels between Big Tech and Standard Oil is the growing influence of their product. By the time of Standard Oil's mandatory break-up, oil was assuming a much larger role on the world stage. The automobile age was just beginning. It would become a dominant economic force in the following decades, with all of those cars powered by gasoline, then all of those airplanes. For decades, oil was the dominant fuel to heat homes. If Rockefeller had maintained his control over the oil business as the decades went by, he would have been the most powerful man on earth.

With tech companies, data is the new oil. Thirty years ago, data was valuable, but it was fairly crude, and its uses were relatively unsophisticated. Few people realized that controlling data produced by internet-based services, advertising, and information exchange would lead to control of the internet or, indeed, that data would become the main currency of power around the world, as well as a threat to our privacy and democracy. We now know that the relationship between data collection, control, and its distribution and sale are critical to competition and future innovation. That's why Big Tech's thirst for data is only increasing.

As with oil, the companies that control data assets will be the gatekeepers to the new economy, and ultimately too powerful. Oil became the catalyst for dozens of economic conflicts as well as some real wars. Who knows if data will ever mobilize armies, but it has already mobilized hackers and led to cyberwars. This trend shows no sign of easing up.

The role of Big Tech as gatekeeper in the new economy was the central focus of the U.S. Department of Justice's challenge to Google, which was announced just prior to the 2020 U.S. presidential election. You know it's important when an issue gets bipartisan support in the midst of the most divisive election in modern history. The Justice Department described Google as a "monopoly gatekeeper to the internet." The implications and what's at stake are very clear. The key to a vibrant and open economy is captured in the simple notion that there always must be an opportunity for a better mousetrap to enter and win in the market. If that does not hold true, it's a warning that key aspects of a free society are in jeopardy. It means merit does not get rewarded. It means the rich will only get richer, and that there will be a concentration of power. It means fewer checks and balances across the economic, social, and ultimately political spectrum. This is not a class warfare issue: this is a free society issue. Free societies are agnostic about who comes out on top. They are about what the winners have done to earn society's rewards and winning once does not entitle us to win again.

We are all entitled to the chance to "win." The very essence of this opportunity, what was once colloquially referred to as the "American Dream," is what makes life in free societies vibrant, fun, resilient, and successful. When the best ideas can't find a path to survival because they are blocked, it means meritorious competition is no longer picking the winners and losers. Ensuring that neither governments nor private companies pick the winners and losers is fundamental to a properly functioning marketplace.

Big Tech platforms can't be allowed to squelch competitive entry and innovation, whether by merely buying up all their competitors or abusing their dominant positions to "win" with consumers. That could mean potentially breaking them up. At minimum, there needs to be greater transparency about how they do business. Markets function better with better information. There also needs to be protection of consumer privacy, and regulation to prevent the spread of misinformation.

The art of competition enforcement is context. For instance, Apple and Google arranged a deal in which Google was made the default search engine on Apple's default Safari browser; this sort of situation is often given the benefit of the doubt. These deals are considered fine until they aren't. If the major platforms become so big there is no opportunity for a more innovative mousetrap to surface, that's a problem. And it happens. These platforms become victims of their own success, and must acknowledge that with size comes more power and therefore more responsibility in a free society.

Even if Big Tech platforms are broken up, there could be a silver lining for them and their shareholders. The breakup of Standard Oil created thirty-four independent companies, including ExxonMobil, Chevron, and ConocoPhillips, and it made Rockefeller the world's first billionaire. When asked about the breakup, President Roosevelt said, "No wonder Wall Street's prayer now is: 'Oh Merciful Providence, give us another dissolution.'" At least in a democracy, even when the government is united against you, you can still get rewarded for your hard work.

*

The power of media to manipulate is as old as media itself. In 1938, radio was the most immediate form of mass communication, with millions sitting in their living rooms, all listening to the same show. On October 30, 1938, a young actor and director named Orson Welles narrated a version of H. G. Wells' 1898 novel *The War of the Worlds*, which featured an alien invasion. His narration was interrupted by seemingly live reports of a Martian invasion in New Jersey, which involved aliens attacking with heat rays. A spaceship landed in Manhattan and released poison gas. The reporter relating this new to the audience coughed, then the line went dead. These vérité touches led some listeners to believe there was an actual alien invasion happening. The next day, there was outrage in the newspapers, calling for regulation by the Federal Communications Commission. A medium as important and ubiquitous as radio shouldn't be used to stoke the fears of the nation, they argued.

Today the internet is the most dominant form of media interaction, and there is a new alien invasion, only this time it's real. The Russians have manipulated the media, not unlike Welles, and convinced thousands of people of something that never happened.

We ultimately settled on rules for radio, print, and television broadcasting, and we will one day figure out the rules for internet communications. The pillars of those rules will be more sophisticated approaches to competition and market dominance, privacy, copyright, liability, and political campaign laws. As the digital world evolves, we will need to build consensus around the rules of the road for this all-encompassing digital highway. The answers won't come easily, but we need to agree on the questions. Our challenge is to ensure we can find the right balance to curb the excesses while preserving and continuing to encourage the innovation we all want to see.

When we look at Big Tech acquisitions of smaller players and what are called "killer acquisitions," we need to look at potential competition issues. We must consider the potential capacity of a smaller platform rather than its market penetration at the time of its acquisition. Maybe it is not such a small acquisition in digital and innovation terms after all, and its acquisition by a giant platform actually shouldn't be allowed, the way Facebook's acquisition of Instagram was.

We also need to redefine and reassess what constitutes uniquely anti-competitive conduct in the digital world. Amazon was accused of luring resellers into their marketplace and then using the information from their clients' sales to determine whether Amazon wanted to enter that very same market to compete against them. This was allegedly the case with Diaper.com.

Amazon's own documents revealed they were willing to lose $200 million per month on diapers to eliminate competition and then raise prices later. Talk about putting a massive iceberg in your path. At the very least, Amazon should be forced to disclose this strategy to potential resellers on their platform; you are welcome to join the Amazon platform but be aware we may use your information to compete against you later. Let the market dictate how many will join under those terms.

Regarding privacy, before the digital world, we could never have imagined someone could actually know more about us than we know about ourselves and have data to prove it. But now it is true. We all have unconscious biases, which means that we tend to see ourselves and our worlds as we want to see them, not how they are. Facebook and Google have no illusions about us: they know what we like and don't like, what we do and don't do, in terms of cold hard data. For the first time in history, private actors know more about the citizenry than their governments. While blanket trust in government is not healthy either, it is a function of the devil you know, and the fact that at least every once in a while, we have the opportunity to throw them out. But how many of us vote at the Facebook or Google annual shareholders' meeting? This is a frightening proposition. In the digital world, this information will become more known, and we will have to decide who we ultimately trust to have it and how much of it is collected.

We will also need to revisit our internet liability laws. With the use of Artificial Intelligence technology, digital platforms increasingly have better knowledge of what is on their sites. They need to govern their sites more responsibly or else we can only assume that they are knowingly distributing harmful content. We already have rules on what a newspaper can print and what can be aired on TV. There is an argument that digital platforms, like the phone companies, merely facilitate discussions between users, and are not the publishers of that content and therefore don't have to take responsibility for it. While aspects of that may be true, the phone companies don't and can't instantly broadcast conversations among millions of users across the globe in the way that digital platforms can. We have well over a century of court rulings on what is offensive content or hate speech. We need to better apply these standards of human conduct, not to mention political advertising and campaign rules, to the digital world. No amount of digital progress is worth our democracy.

Corporations can't be relied upon to be the defenders of democracy. Historically, corporations resist any oversight or government interference. They are commercial enterprises, naturally driven by profit. On the internet, profit comes from advertising, which is driven by numbers, which are augmented by clickbait. It doesn't matter how unbalanced, hate-filled, or racist the message: if it attracts eyeballs, it can pay. Unchecked, the main digital platforms could become forums filled with hyperbolic messages and extreme voices. This has already begun to happen, and these divisions will leave us weaker. They also can be used by foreign adversaries to further weaken us further, raising important national security implications. The global platform that attracts the most attention can charge the most for advertising. It will be a race to the bottom as audiences get more and more desensitized, and seek a progressively more extreme clickbait "fix." This is why some regulation is necessary to monitor and curb excesses, protecting the larger societal gameboard for us all.

In a free and civilized society, the whole of our rights must be greater than the individual parts. If we all pursue unbounded and maximum personal rights, there is a point when these individual rights will actually begin to diminish. As we chart the course ahead, we must have reasonable expectations for our own demands and leave room for others and their opinions, or we risk getting sucked into the black hole of a concept of freedom that will consume us all.

Chapter Eleven

The Game of Broken Politics

W E SEE MANY CHALLENGES AROUND US. Our politics and social fabric are fracturing, there is growing economic disruption and anxiety, continued battles between urban and rural, rising alienation in the western world, increasing environmental threats, and global pandemics, just to name a few. Our democracy has faced greater challenges, and somehow each generation passed on an even better way of life to the next. This is the unwritten promise that each generation implicitly makes to the next. Whether it was our war efforts, universal healthcare and social safety net, or our special cultural mosaic, each required a forged consensus. Building a new consensus will be the first part of our own test, and it will define the Canada we leave for our children.

Consensus doesn't mean unanimity, an impossible standard in a free society (as my own family dinners testify). But there should be a consensus of a vast majority of Canadians, beyond any political definitions, when it comes to sharing a vision of Canada that will create shared prosperity for us all, and not just a few. Fortunately, we live in an age where technology has democratized the tools of productivity and economic participation, so we all have a chance to plug our passions and energy into the market to be able to reach for the Canadian dream. We just need a consensus framework that prioritizes the potential of the individual rather than an industry, and breaks away from the paradigms that defined the last economic revolution.

However, what we are seeing around us are deep divisions and partisanship conflicts that threaten to fray our society. Knowing how we got trapped in this maze of division and partisanship can help us get back out. One of our biggest problems is how we play the game of modern party politics.

From a competition and game theory perspective, there may be an explanation for why the major political parties are taking us into more partisan terrain. The result is elections that become pitched battles between the extreme left or right, with rhetoric to match. These narratives can have a lasting impact and make necessary consensus even harder to reach post-election. They are like harsh words said in the heat of a marital dispute; your partner can't unhear those words afterwards when you realize the relationship is worth saving.

But what has happened to give those partisan narratives enough oxygen to be sustained? The majority of Canadians, as a friend of mine, John Stackhouse, once noted, are radically centrist. But we may be in danger of losing that. One reason could be political expediency: you need to cater to your base in order to get and hold power. This would replace the hard work of building a consensus, which history tells us is the best way to deal with national challenges. It's hard to win the Stanley Cup if half the team is benched.

Some of this is due to modern data mining and being able to use targeted information to zero in on individual voters or voter blocks, slice and dice them, and cater to special interests to win a crucial riding or leadership campaign. Because of the skewed nomination rules for the Conservative party, Andrew Scheer did it by catering to Quebec dairy farmers, and reports of Erin O'Toole's campaign targeting Quebec gun club members.

The major political parties are increasingly unable to break away from their hardcore bases. The federal New Democratic Party and Conservative Party seem to be the two strongest examples of this. The NDP has never formed the government, and the Conservative Party has had one majority government since 1993.

While the Liberals have done better in holding the centre, there is increasing pressure from its base to move left. Looking through the lens of game theory, these parties become more and more captured by their base as they seek support each time an election comes around.

To illustrate, Jack and Jill play a schoolyard game to see who can make the most friends. They have rich parents who give them an unlimited allowance, and they quickly discover that it's easier to make "friends" when you buy them things. So, there is the moral hazard of relying on buying things to make friends, which starts a gifting arms race. But it also produces expectations among their existing friends. How much do they value their friendship? If you agreed to give me one chocolate bar a year to be your friend, but then you give two bars to your new friends, there is friction. This approach to politics doesn't result in a broadly representative and consensus-driven government that can best respond to real problems. We will all get more chocolate bars if we work together to build a bigger, better chocolate factory. It is likely that more competition for the political centre could help to rejuvenate our politics.

I have noticed that open competition, even in the most dominant markets, always helps innovators to better respond to and meet the demands of the customers they ultimately serve. This equally applies to a government and the demands of its citizens. Henry Ford once said that when it came to his Model T, the customer can have any colour they want, as long as it's black. This worked until competition arrived in a variety of colours. Markets rule because over time, like democracies, they must reflect the will of the people. This happens through a continuous process of furnishing and course-correcting. We generally don't like to spend our hard-earned money on garbage. We don't enjoy being ripped off. If we feel that political groups are ripping us off in the same way, we will feel that they are no longer serving our needs and we will stop buying whatever they are selling us.

We need to resist slipping further into this spiral of partisanship and gamesmanship, where consensus only gets more out of reach. My family history, my personal experiences, and my legal career have forced me to always at least try to see the world through the eyes of another. I believe it has made me a better lawyer, neighbour, and parent and, along the way, built bridges and created consensus. Being able to see the other side and empathize with one another is the foundation of the consensus upon which we can create the most inclusive and prosperous Canada yet.

Chapter Twelve
Fast in the 6

I T WAS OVER A FAMILY DINNER, while watching the divisive rhetoric of the 2016 U.S. election, that my wife Lisa and I thought we had to do something, anything, to resist what we saw as the false logic of Trump's campaign rhetoric. Voters were angry and anxious and there was genuine inequality to deal with, yet they voted to increase anger, anxiety, and inequality. How was that going to make things great?

Worldwide, we had observed the rise of similar "populist" movements and wondered whether they could take hold in Canada. Populism on any end of the political spectrum can be dangerous. The simplicity of a populist message is good at capturing raw emotions, but ultimately doesn't offer real solutions to real problems. It leads to political sectarianism that excludes rather than unites. Like many, Lisa and I wondered what this century will bring for our children, and how we might resist the worst outcome.

How about having everyone over for dinner?

By everyone, we meant all of Toronto. A public dinner with neighbours of every creed, color, and faith. A reminder of the strength and power of unity that comes from enjoying our differences. Of course, our backyard wasn't big enough to host the whole city, so we asked Mayor John Tory if we could host it on the enormous Nathan Phillips Square at City Hall. He quickly and enthusiastically jumped on board, and has remained supportive. This free dinner, open to the public and staged at City Hall, would be our form of resistance.

But we also needed something to share and celebrate. We decided to share an experience special to Muslims but that reflected something that Muslims have in common with many faiths. Ramadan, the Muslim month of fasting, was coming up; when the sun goes down during Ramadan, everyone gets together to break their fast and enjoy a big meal. The act of fasting is common to many religions and cultures, so this seemed like the perfect occasion to bring everyone together to share a meal.

The act of fasting is common to many faiths and cultures, so we felt that inviting others to celebrate a breaking of the fast would be a way to enjoy our differences within a familiar tradition. It was designed to be a multi-faith celebration, in the spirit of the Santa Claus parades put on each Christmas in cities across North America.

Lisa and I came up with the name Fast in the 6 because of local Toronto superstar Drake, who uses the "6" handle for Toronto (derived from the area code 416) in his chart-topping songs. Lisa and our four kids listened to Drake constantly in the family car, and with all of our kids in sports—hockey, soccer, and rowing—we tended to spend a lot of time in the car. We shared the name Fast in the 6 with everyone and they loved it.

Lisa and I believed this would be an event about making people feel a certain way, and that it could only be pulled off by people who themselves felt that way. For the event's motto, we chose the words Diversity.Unity.Prosperity. It expressed what we were feeling and captured a forward-looking narrative.

Lisa and I are both lawyers and had no event planning experience, so we were starting from scratch. It was lucky we didn't know what we were getting into. If we had realized how much work it would take, we may not have done it. But we are blessed with a wonderful network of friends from every background, race, and religion, and they helped us to make it happen.

We decided that the best way to get people to attend would be to hold a free, public event that would include a meal, entertainment, and a fireworks display. We knew we'd need real event planning expertise, marketing, and, of course, sponsorship funds.

Throughout my career, I have been blessed to work with many clients who became personal friends along the way. To me, this is what defines a genuinely rewarding career: being lucky enough to do what you like while also having the good fortune of serving people who become friends. All businesses are ultimately about serving people. The more we feel that connection, the more fulfilling our work. Fortunately, I had made connections over the years in each of the areas where we needed expertise.

The first step was working with the city's event planning team to confirm a date at Nathan Phillips Square. At the time, a friend and actor, Zaib Shaikh, was the city's Film Commissioner and Director of Entertainment Industries. In his role of Imam Amaar in the hit series Little Mosque on the Prairie, he had played a major part in giving Canadians a connection to their Muslim neighbours. He understood the potential of this event, and he and his wife Kirstine Stewart, who among many other accomplishments once led Twitter in Canada, helped get us started.

We diligently filled out the many forms (this was one place our lawyerly skills really helped—we are good at forms) and set the date of June 9, 2017 for the inaugural Fast in the 6. The relief of securing a date was immediately replaced by the challenge of turning an idea into reality. With the help of an amazing city event planning team led by Harold Mah, we began drawing up plans and organizing meetings, putting together detailed checklists for each component of the event, whether food or security or something else. Lisa and I then created a master checklist we could methodically work through to make sure we were on track. The lists brought some order to the chaos and a sense of progress as we checked off each item.

For me, the night wouldn't be fun unless it ended in fireworks. I have fond memories of what used to be the Benson & Hedges fireworks event on the Toronto waterfront, where the lavish display was set to music. I mistakenly thought it would be easy to replicate. I assumed it was simply a matter of writing "fireworks" into the evening's program. Our first obstacle was city council. It had never heard of Fast in the 6, and wondered why we wanted to have fireworks on Nathan Phillips Square? It also wanted to know if there was a precedent. Had any private event been allowed a firework display in the past? The council couldn't recall one. Fortunately, we learned that fireworks had been approved for World Pride Day celebrations in 2007. Council approved our request.

We finally had all the necessary approvals. Now we needed money. The network of community leaders I'd met in my years on Bay Street was helpful. I sat down with a long list of friends to tell them what we were planning. I had met Chrystia Freeland, then Foreign Minister, when I was president of the Canadian Club and had hosted her and the Prime Minister. I asked if she would speak at our event. I had also met Michael Medline, the President of Sobeys, when we were both trapped in the Chicago airport for hours, waiting for a delayed fight. I asked if he would supply food for the event. Blake Hutcheson, who was president of Oxford Properties, is a friend and neighbour, and I asked for his support. I also received support from philanthropists like Mohammad and Najla Al-Zaibak. Each of these people immediately understood and supported the values represented by Fast in the 6 and enthusiastically signed on to help. The final list of corporate supporters for that first event included TD Bank, Maple Lodge Farms, Oxford Properties, Sobeys, RBC, Air Canada, and my firm, Torys LLP. It was Maple Lodge Farms and Sobeys that generously supplied the food to the thousands who came to that first event to share in the breaking of the fast.

For entertainment, we lined up a varied slate that included the Toronto Symphony Orchestra, comedian Mo Amer, musical guest Yuna, and Mustafa the Poet. The event was hosted by a dear friend, Raptors home game host and radio personality Mark Strong. If you've ever been to a Raptors home game, you know the energy, warmth and sheer fun he brings to anything he touches. We wanted the entertainment to be as diverse as the audience.

In addition to Chrystia Freeland, we planned to include remarks from Mayor John Tory, and a message from Ontario Premier Kathleen Wynne. We wanted to bring our private and public realms together in this common cause. Other politicians wanted to speak, but we decided to limit it to one representative from each level of government. We wanted the event to be about the guests, not politics.

The heaviest responsibility we had was ensuring the security of our guests. Planning this event was a microcosm of life: we had to balance ideals with pragmatism. We would never be able to forgive ourselves if something unthinkable happened because we were not prepared. With that in mind, we planned for the worst and hoped for the best. We didn't know who might try to disrupt things or, God forbid, something worse. One extreme racist—I was reminded of the Wolves of Odin—or even an extremist Muslim could be a danger to everyone there. In addition to city security staff and Toronto Police officers, we hired private security to ensure we created a safe space for our guests to enjoy the event. Fortunately, in the four years of the event, we have always seen the best of Toronto and its people.

After all our planning, the next big anxiety was the weather. What would it be like on that day? No matter how much time and effort we'd put into it, it was an outdoor event, and if the weather didn't cooperate, we were toast. For about a month before the event, every Friday's weather had been a disaster, and I wondered whether our Friday would be cursed, too. But on Friday, June 9, we woke to a beautiful day. My anxiety then shifted to the event's attendance. We had built it. Would they come?

I had to go to the office for most of the day, so I was getting second-hand reports on the set-up. People sent me pictures as the stage and venues were being put up. I had been to many events, and it always looked like they just magically appeared and disappeared. I had never appreciated the logistics and effort required until now. Everything from the placement of each food venue, to the stage, the fireworks, entrances, exits, and crowd control barriers had to be accounted for. On top of all that, every delivery to Nathan Phillips Square had to be coordinated, so there wasn't chaos. It was like an elaborate dance to make everything work. The formal event program was to start at 8 p.m. but we were having a small reception an hour earlier to thank our sponsors and volunteers. It was a long day of setting up and a longer day of anticipating who would show up.

I got to Nathan Phillips Square around 5 p.m. and the set-up was almost complete. Last minute issues were dealt with as they came up. People started to trickle in, but by the time we went into City Hall to attend our sponsor reception, it wasn't a large crowd. My anxiety was building.

Once inside, we could no longer see what was happening outside. We went around and thanked our sponsors and volunteers. Lisa and I were regularly interrupted by volunteers asking if we could spare a moment to speak to a TV reporter from this or that news outlet. Each time we ran out to do an interview, we saw the crowd getting bigger. It was kind of like watching popcorn popping. More and more people materialized, seemingly out of nowhere. At 8:30, we came out onto the stage to welcome the crowd and looked out at Nathan Phillips Square to see thousands of people of every colour and creed. Approximately 7,500 people showed up, and all the major news outlets were there.

Mayor John Tory and Chrystia Freeland gave short, heartfelt speeches. We had asked them to keep things short, knowing that the sun was setting at 8:50, and we would have to break the fast then. We also didn't want our guests to feel they were being lectured to. I have been to so many events in my life where one long, well-intended speech gave way to another and you could feel the impatience build in the audience. We wanted to make sure our event was more experience than words. That meant a hard stop to the speeches after twenty minutes.

The speeches ended, the fast was broken, and a children's choir sang O Canada accompanied by a Toronto Symphony Orchestra ensemble. The ensemble continued to play several beautiful pieces as people enjoyed the free food. We had poetry from Mustafa the Poet, a young, up-and-coming Toronto poet championed by Drake. He was followed by Mo Amer, probably the best-known Muslim comedian in North America (he would later go on to have a hit special on Netflix and has joined us every year since). Then we had the beautiful music of Yuna, a chart-topping Muslim artist with her hit song "Crush," which she had recorded with megastar Usher. We ended the night with a massive fireworks display set off from the roof of City Hall. It went high into the night sky, set to beautiful music, and could be seen from far away. Lisa and I had spent hours listening to pieces of orchestral music to try and find the right movements to capture the feelings we wanted people to leave with at the end of the night.

What a night it was, so beautiful and so warm and embracing of all who came and enjoyed. In so many ways, we didn't want it to end, but we also knew that short and sweet is always best, so by 10:30 it was over. As the fireworks ended, we felt exhausted but elated. When we got home, we turned on the local CP24 news channel to see the coverage of the event and the fireworks at the top of every hour.

In the days that followed, we heard from people who had attended. Tourists from the U.S. and Germany remarked that they wouldn't see a similar event on such a scale in their home-towns, with people of different backgrounds enjoying an evening together and nothing more being asked of them. A group called the Voices of Toronto, an initiative of a dear friend, Susan Farrow, and co-founder Jennifer Pernfuss, had created a display at our event and encouraged people to fill out cards, writing down how they felt about Toronto. More than 1,000 people took the time to fill out cards with inspiring, beautiful messages and we read them all. They were later turned into a book. Chrystia Freeland told me that she'd tell other foreign ministers about Fast in the 6 as an example of Canada's diverse, inclusive society.

We knew a lot of people had showed up for the food. Maple Lodge Farms told us they participated in a lot of community events, but few had the cross-section of people they had seen that even-ing. For them, it was about much more than giving away free food, which they generously do several times a year at other events. They were introduced to an amazing representation of Canada, which made both their social and business case for joining the event only stronger. They, along with Sobeys, have been a corner-stone of the event ever since.

*

When I was twelve-years-old, I spent a year living in Slave Lake, helping my father. He had just bought a new retail business. It was 1982, and the Alberta oil boom had gone bust. He'd been in real estate, but had lost a lot when oil prices collapsed. He had to start over in a new business that was 210 kilometres north of our home in Edmonton. Being a big family of six kids, and my father didn't want to take us out of our schools and disrupt our childhoods. But as the eldest, I felt it would be fun to move up there for a year to help out. I could also play hockey out there.

I learned a lot of lessons from my father, including resilience. One critical lesson I learned is that in the retail business, you need to think about what the customer wants rather than what you want, which requires seeing things from the eyes of another person. Every once in a while, he would let me buy something for the store that I really liked but that he knew wouldn't sell. He did it just to show me at the end of the season that they were still on the rack. His point was to prove that thinking only of yourself ultimately doesn't pay. Those lessons stuck.

Now, as a competition lawyer who studies markets and consumer behaviour, I'm still asking that question: is there a market for that and what value does it offer others? I have seen many good ideas, products, and plans, but they ultimately don't mean much if people don't actually buy them. The only real test is to open the doors and see who will come and "buy." That experience rarely lies to you. People came to Fast in the 6 and have continued to come, which told us that we were not the only ones who wanted to resist division, who wanted to find a path forward together. We realized the real joy in what we were doing was not leading anything but rather tapping into something. We were grateful to have given it a platform.

One of the other aspects of Fast in the 6 was the opportunity to celebrate our unique Canadian Muslim identity, one that had been shaped over a century. While I am proud of my Lebanese heritage, it cannot supplant my identity as a Canadian of Muslim faith. Like other faiths, Islam has different complexions in different places. I reached out to many in my Muslim community network to build consensus about an evolving Canadian Muslim identity. Not everyone was on board. One potential corporate sponsor appointed a well-meaning older employee, who was Muslim, to discuss whether they would support us. This representative told me the event wouldn't work; it was too different from the Ramadan events he had supported in the past. He was certain his CEO would get complaints from Muslim customers if we held the event. As it turned out, the opposite happened. In fact, one of the most powerful messages we received from young Muslim Canadians who attended is that this event was the first time they felt the Muslim identity was part of the Canadian fabric. They now look forward to it every year.

Fast in the 6 came to life in Toronto in 2017 with the same spirit that built that first mosque in Edmonton. To the south of us, there was a "Muslim ban," but on that evening we had Diversity. Unity.Prosperity. Humanity has collectively written, experienced, and sacrificed too much to go back to where we started: local tribes, brawn over brains, fear over hope. Fast in the 6 serves as a reminder that Canada remains a special place that embraces everyone, just as it did my great-grandfather decades ago. If we want to build on Canada's specialness and capitalize on all of our potential, the times demand we both embrace our tribal instinct for self-preservation while also recognizing that humanity is now our tribe. It is the best means of collective survival in the modern age.

Epilogue

C AN A TIMELINE TELL A STORY? As a born and bred Albertan who happens to be Muslim, it seems surreal to be watching a part of my identity being portrayed as the "other." In that light, the years 1867, 1938, 2012, and 2021 speak to me.

1867: We live in the greatest country on earth and you just have to pick up a newspaper on any given day and read what's happening in other parts of the world to remind you of that. It didn't happen by accident. While nowhere near perfect, especially with regard to the treatment of Indigenous peoples, the founding of the country in 1867 did carve out a place for both the English and French cultures. In modern history, it's hard to find countries where past conflicts were not allowed to define the future character of a nation, and where minority rights were both protected and promoted.

1938: My great-grandfather and the early Canadian Muslim community he belonged to came together to build the first mosque in Canada. It was not built by an insular community in isolation, but with the support and generosity of non-Muslim Albertans. It really was the first little mosque on the prairie. That mosque is now literally a part of history, preserved and relocated to Fort Edmonton Park as a testament to its historical significance.

The Lebanese roots that helped build the mosque echo to this day. In the immediate aftermath of the port explosion in Beirut in August 2020, I wrote an op-ed in the *Toronto Star* titled "Lebanon Must Rise Again to be a Source of Beauty." I wanted to start a conversation about how, as Canadians, we could seek to engage Lebanon and the broader global issues it represented. I got a call from the Prime Minister the next day. The first thing he said was that he had been to "Lac Lafarge." I immediately knew he meant to say "Lac La Biche," and corrected him, but the fact he mis-spoke meant he wasn't just reading from prepared notes. He said he had enjoyed meeting the generations of Lebanese Canadians who lived there. This is the town where my Uncle Jimmy had his mink ranch in the 1950s, where my father first came when he arrived in Canada, and I still have extended family there. I made the point that because Lebanon was a small country, our dollars could have a big impact and help to and amplify Canada's voice on the world stage. By that evening the government increased our commitment to Lebanon by $25 million. Foreign Affairs Minister François-Philippe Champagne became only the second senior western government representative to visit Beirut, after President Macron of France.

Lebanon has great potential, but it is also an object lesson. Historically, it has shared many traits with Canada: multicultural, multilingual, a generosity that accepts refugees and engages with foreigners. Outside forces have shaped Lebanon over the centuries, but ultimately, its undoing came from within. Religious intolerance and sectarianism caused the deaths of tens of thousands, left one of the world's most beautiful cities in ruins, and impacted the lives of two generations of Lebanese people. No one benefitted and almost everyone suffered.

Ninety years ago, when the mosque was built in Edmonton, there were fewer than 1,000 Muslims in Canada. Now there are more than a million. Yet it seems sometimes as if we are regressing. In the wake of the debate in Quebec about its charter of values, a Quebec mosque was sprayed with pig's blood and the words "integrate or go home" were written on it. What if you're *already* home? In my mind, it is the vandals who need to integrate. They are compromising the Canadian values that allow all of us to practice our faiths and cultures, the values that make this such an extraordinary country. They may think they are "protecting" their idea of Quebec culture (which in my experience is one of warmth and appreciation for life), but sectarianism is often born out of a misguided sense of cultural pride rather than hate.

2012: About eighty-five years after my great-grandfather came to Canada to make a life for himself and future generations, I got to watch my son, his great-great-grandson, carry the Canadian flag in the opening ceremonies of the 100th Anniversary of the Grey Cup on behalf of all Canadian youth. As a father from Edmonton who grew up loving the CFL and this great country, I thought of my great-grandfather and the immense embrace Canada had shown him, and I hope that it continues to embrace those who come here for a better life.

2021: The COVID-19 pandemic and the digital revolution converged to change our lives irrevocably almost overnight. Our vulnerabilities were suddenly exposed. The virus accelerated our transition to the digital economy and shone a spotlight on where we are least prepared for future growth. And it impacted our most marginalized communities, further exposing our inequities. Technology has democratized the tools of productivity, and now we need to empower the individual rather than big industries. Counting on corporations to open another car plant or expand an oil facility is no longer a wise plan. Socially, the pandemic has reminded us that we are still our brother's keeper. While waiting for the vaccine, we had to rely on Canadian decency, such as sticking to the protocols of wearing a mask and keeping our social distance, to get us through the long months of lockdown with our country in one piece.

Although the challenges of the modern age seem daunting, my path has shown me that there is always an opportunity for my voice to be heard. There is always a way to appeal to our cherished institutions to ever so slightly, and often much too slowly, move toward a just society. We don't need to demolish our history to build our future. To face our current challenges and opportunities, we need collectively to build and expand on our diverse strengths to reach new heights and pass on an even better Canada to our children. The Raptors represented that and brought us together during the Spring of 2019. Who knew Canada could become a basketball country, too? They became Canada's team for that magical year and united East and West, black, white, and brown, and commanded the world stage on all our behalf. They gave us an example of something new to love without diminishing our pride in our oldest sporting tradition, hockey, and reminded us of the power and potential of unity.

This book is rooted in the tradition of saying please and thank you and standing in line because these values remain an enduring creed to build upon and rally around. It symbolizes Canada. A place where you respect and are respected, and where everyone, rich or poor, big or small, white or black, new or old, are expected to play by the same rules and no one is above the law. It captures our dreams of equity, opportunity, and hope with an inclusive meritocracy as our north star, and it doesn't ask who we are in our journey toward what we can all be.